How to Fe...

WELBECK
BALANCE

About the Author

Ruth Kudzi has been coaching for well over a decade and has run an award-winning coaching business since 2016. In 2019 Ruth opened the Optimus Coach Academy where she trains and certifies others to become coaches. The academy has certified over 500 people; and worked with hundreds more within organizations and through CPD programs.

Ruth combines over 28 years of experience studying Psychology and Neuroscience with a BA in Psychology and Management, MA in Psychology and Education and PGCERT in Coaching and Psychology. She is committed to her own personal development: she has a raft of qualifications in coaching and associated fields, including diplomas in Positive Psychology, Neuroscience, Small Business Coaching, Personal Coaching, Executive Coaching and Neuroscience for leadership alongside being a Spiral Energy Coach, an NLP Practitioner and a DISC Level 3 Trainer. She has also trained in mindfulness, nutrition and CBT and has worked with mentors, teachers and coaches from all over the world to strengthen and deepen her practice.

The Optimus Coach Academy is at the forefront of international training, with students from over 30 different countries learning evidence-based solutions-focused coaching with its roots in Neuroscience and Psychology.

How to Feel Better

4 Steps to Self-Coach Your Way to
a Happier, More Authentic Life

Ruth Kudzi

WELBECK
BALANCE

Published in 2023 by Welbeck Balance
An imprint of Welbeck Non-Fiction Limited
Part of Welbeck Publishing Group
Offices in: London – 20 Mortimer Street, London W1T 3JW &
Sydney – 205 Commonwealth Street, Surry Hills 2010
www.welbeckpublishing.com

A CIP catalogue record for this book is available from the British Library.

ISBN
978-1-80129-258-0

Typeset by Lapiz Digital Services
Printed in Great Britain by CPI Group (UK) Ltd, Croydon CR0 4YY

10 9 8 7 6 5 4 3 2 1

Note/Disclaimer
Welbeck encourages and welcomes diversity and different viewpoints. However, all
views, thoughts, and opinions expressed in this book are the author's own and are not
necessarily representative of Welbeck Publishing Group as an organization. Welbeck
Publishing Group makes no representations or warranties of any kind, express or implied,
with respect to the accuracy, completeness, suitability or currency of the contents of this
book, and specifically disclaims, to the extent permitted by law, any implied warranties of
merchantability or fitness for a particular purpose and any injury, illness, damage, death,
liability or loss incurred, directly or indirectly from the use or application of any of the
information contained in this book. This book is solely intended for informational purposes
and guidance only and is not intended to replace, diagnose, treat or act as a substitute for
professional and expert medical and/or psychiatric advice. The author and the publisher
are not medical practitioners nor counsellors and professional advice should be sought
before embarking on any health-related programme.

Any names, characters, trademarks, service marks and trade names detailed in this book
are the property of their respective owners and are used solely for identification and
reference purposes. This book is a publication of Welbeck Non-Fiction, part of
Welbeck Publishing Group and has not been licensed, approved, sponsored or
endorsed by any person or entity.

Every reasonable effort has been made to trace copyright holders of material
produced in this book, but if any have been inadvertently overlooked the
publishers would be glad to hear from them.

My biggest driver for wanting to feel better came from having my two daughters and wanting to be a role model for them.

This book is dedicated to Jessica and Sophia and to my husband Christian who has helped me to stay on track throughout the whole process and is my biggest supporter.

Contents

Introduction

Before we dive in, allow me to introduce myself: I'm an educator at heart and currently run a coach training academy alongside my own coaching business, and prior to this I was a senior leader within education. I've been pretty obsessed with human behaviour for as long as I can remember and first studied Psychology in 1994. I have a Masters in Psychology, alongside a whole raft of qualifications and training in different aspects of coaching. I am one of fewer than 70 Master Certified Coaches in the UK (International Coaching Federation Accredited). I will be sharing my own lived experience and journey alongside what I have learned along the way as a coach, trainer and teacher.

What if I told you that the secret to feeling better is not an expensive gym membership or green smoothies (don't get me wrong, these also help), but coaching? From the years of work I have done personally, and with thousands of clients as a coach, trainer and educator, I know that coaching has the power to change how you think and feel about yourself and transform your world from the inside out. The reason the coaching industry is booming is because it is a powerful life-changing technique, and the good news is that by using this book you can discover how to coach yourself!

Self-awareness is the driving catalyst for change, which is why it is at the heart of my self-coaching method. Using tried-and-tested exercises, you will be exploring your thoughts, emotions and behaviour, enabling you to get clarity on what you want and then taking action to get there.

This is your time to commit to feeling better, creating that plan and making the necessary changes to get the things you desire. You are going to learn to recognize the patterns and behaviours that have been keeping you stuck, and start exploring that inner world of feelings and thoughts that often makes you feel not good enough.

As you go through the book, you will learn my simple four-step self-coaching process. You can use this simple repeatable formula time and time again to coach yourself to success:

- **Step One:** Assess where you currently are
- **Step Two:** Get clear on where you want to be
- **Step Three:** Make a plan to take you forward
- **Step Four:** Integrate and embed the change

All the approaches I use are rooted in evidence from psychology and neuroscience, combined with ideas informed by energetics, somatics and psychodynamics. This integration of different schools of thought is something I am passionate about, as I believe when you expose yourself to various paradigms it can build a deeper knowledge and help you to see yourself in a more holistic way.

Throughout the book I am going to refer to some key concepts that underpin how coaching works, explaining their origins and how you can apply them to your life to feel better. These approaches are all evidence-based and are techniques that I have used personally, both in my role as a coach and in my training school, where I have worked with thousands of clients. The book follows the curriculum map I use at my training academy, Optimus: nearly every tool and technique has a research base behind it and is built on the principles of neuroplasticity and the brain's organizing principle of threat/reward.

Key concepts

Neuroplasticity refers to the brain's ability to change and grow by building new neural pathways: evidence from brain scanning shows that you can effectively re-wire your brain through learning and repetition. This links to the concept of growth mindset proposed by psychologist Carol Dweck, which states that when you believe you can improve and get better you are likely to! Finally, the brain's organizing principle is proposed by Evian Gordon, psychologist and founder of Total Brain, who states that as humans we are hardwired to move away from pain and toward pleasure.

These key concepts are at the heart of self-coaching and integrate with the different modalities that I will introduce you to. At Optimus, the coaches take a holistic approach and always remain curious with their clients. I encourage you to be curious too. It is a skill I encourage everyone to nurture because when you are curious about what is going on for you and your reactions, you learn more. Equally, when you are curious about other people and their situations, you often start to see the world through a different lens.

This is about moving away from black-and-white, all-or-nothing thinking, and leaning into the grey to see what is really going on underneath. The more personal development work I have done, the more I have realized that the concept of "right" and "wrong" or "good" and "bad" is based on perception: most people operate with positive intentions and it is about how we perceive their behaviour, the filters and lens through which we view the world. In this book, and in life, I encourage you to test out different lenses and viewpoints and be open to the fact that your perception may not be reality.

How to use this book

Each of the four sections broadly links to the steps that I shared at the beginning: you will notice that these steps are referenced throughout and I encourage you to build connections between the different parts. The book is designed to be read chronologically, with the themes running through the heart of the writing and learning, but it is also a resource you can dip back into when you are looking for inspiration and support.

Step One: Assess where you currently are

Before you can move forward, you need to establish where you are. The first part of the book focuses on self-discovery and self-awareness, which are at the core of coaching. You are unable to change what you are not aware of. By exploring the here and now, you can deeply connect with the reality of where you are and what you are thinking, feeling and doing. This is a time to take off the mask and dig into you: it may not always be comfortable, so bring your determination and growth mindset.

Step Two: Get clear on where you want to be

The second section of the book is concerned with your big vision for success and what you want to achieve. When you look at this within the context of where you are right now, you will start to see the smaller steps you can take now. In this section you will explore that big dream thinking. When you back it up with action – the smaller steps you can take – it can be the beginning of building new neural pathways. My perspective is to dream the dream and then come back to the here and now, with small steps that bring big results due to their compound effect. You will be exploring how you can effectively re-wire your brain by creating a vision to motivate and inspire you.

Step Three: Make a plan to take you forward

Here I show you how to access the resources needed to make change happen, including your mindset and self-belief. This is about making the journey enjoyable, rather than solely focusing on the destination. It is in this part of the book that things start to get real: remember that the plan you put in place must be something you can execute. Again, my approach is to look at the minimum commitment so you can build on that: this is something BJ Fogg, habit expert, suggests and something I use in my own life. For example, committing to 10 minutes of vigorous exercise each day – my minimum commitment – completely changed how I viewed exercise.

If you want to feel better, it isn't all about sacrifice: I am a big believer in working with the pleasure centres in your brain and looking at positive behaviours rather than negative ones. When you experience pleasure, the neurotransmitter dopamine is released and you start to build a cognitive connection between what you did and that feeling. We are wired to move toward anticipated pleasure, so if you repeat that behaviour it will soon become a preference due to that principle. Enjoying yourself actually works with the brain!

Step Four: Integrate and embed the change

Finally, I show you how to integrate the changes into your life, long-term, by learning how to support your brain and body to embed behavioural change. If you don't keep going, you won't feel the benefits. Consider this a marathon rather than a sprint:

I am all for building behavioural changes the slow and sustained way as I know this is what is going to make it stick. It's that compound effect that works.

A personal journey

The premise of this book is that you can improve and build from wherever you are: this is your personal development journey so, however sh*t it feels right now, rest assured you will start to feel better by the end of the four-step programme. Remember, this is only the beginning. You don't read a book, feel better and that's it – we may be good but we aren't magicians. You need to embed and integrate the learning over time to see change.

Throughout the book, I will be asking you questions and encouraging you to reflect. Doing a reflective practice is what's going to help you strengthen those neural pathways and implement change: remember that the questions are there to support your brain, and give you clarity on your thinking so you have a good idea of what to do next. Self-reflection is one of the keys to learning, which is crucial if you want to feel better.

Maybe there was a catalyst or an event which happened to you: redundancy, the end of a relationship, a big birthday that made you say enough is enough. Or, maybe it was more of a gentle, but persistent niggle that left you feeling that you could be happier if you had more time/energy/space.

When you realize those external things are often manifested inside you – the job you can't switch off from, the nightmare boss, the ex who walked out – you discover that the way you react is all about you and your lens. Coaching enables you to recognize your patterns and where they have come from, as well as looking at how you can respond in more effective ways. Remember that you are a work in progress and the gift of self-awareness and clarity can help you avoid more heartache. It is possible to change.

You have a choice, whether you are going to accept where you are right now as your reality or come on this journey with me to help you create the life that you want to live. Are you ready to step out of your shadows and low points and move into the light and start to be who you want to be?

This works if you go all in and commit. This isn't about the shadows disappearing or you becoming elated about everything in your life. It is about you changing the things that are impacting you the most; this might be starting with the big rocks: work, relationships, money, home or starting with the pebbles and building up. Sometimes addressing the big things can feel like too much, and breaking them down into more manageable chunks is more effective.

Part of self-coaching is about developing a growth mindset: you find the area you want to change and then you commit to improving. Remember, this concept can be applied to more than just our cognitive abilities. When you learn who you are, you can step out of feeling like you need to be in control and disliking yourself and into acceptance and joy.

Disclaimer – you won't be feeling joy the whole time! Life happens: even with the work, there will be people and events you find challenging to navigate and, at times, you won't respond in the most helpful or healthy way. I remember when my dad, an alcoholic, died of liver failure. That weekend I drank more wine than I care to admit. It wasn't the healthiest response, but it was what I needed in that moment. I remember my friends being with me and I still feel very grateful to have that network. Even though I didn't know how to articulate what I needed right then, it was very comforting to have them there.

Self-awareness is key

As you move through this book, you will start to get to know yourself better, understanding what is going on for you cognitively and emotionally in different situations. As mentioned earlier, when we are able to understand ourselves we can start to make changes to how we think, feel and act. If we don't know what is going on, it is a lot harder!

Equally, when we are aware of what drives and motivates us it can help us to see other people's perspectives and viewpoints, which can enhance our communication and relationships. The more you understand yourself, the more you are able to understand others.

KEY POINTS TO REMEMBER

- This is about understanding your brain and body based on evidence-based approaches to behavioural change.
- At the core of the book is growth mindset and neuroplasticity.
- You will be learning about how to work more effectively with your brain's organizing principle.
- Self-coaching starts with self-awareness.
- You will be holding up a mirror to yourself and looking at who you are.
- Start to consider what you would like to be different by the end of the book.
- When you develop your self-coaching techniques, you can keep using them.
- Using this book is just the start of you changing.

STEP ONE

Assess Where You
Currently Are

To answer the question "Where are you now?", the work is project "know yourself". As a Master Certified Coach and trainer, I have helped thousands of clients and one thing I have seen time and time again is the power of self-awareness. You will remain stuck if you don't know who you are or what you want to change. Therefore, the best starting point is for you to know what is going on for you in your external and internal worlds. To help you discover that, I'm going to share with you a sequence of tools, techniques and exercises that follows the curriculum at my coaching academy.

One of the first exercises I use with my clients, and that you can use on yourself, is "The Iceberg". Like an iceberg, your appearance, behaviour and physical environment are the parts of yourself that are visible, but there is much more underneath: your values, beliefs, thoughts and habits. In psychodynamic terms, the things above the iceberg are conscious and those below it are unconscious. Working through the exercises in this section will help you to bring those things which are lying beneath the surface to the top, so you can get clarity and increase your self-awareness.

I recommend trying all the exercises and reflecting on the ones that are most impactful for you. Any resistance can be a good indication that you have uncovered something about yourself. If you can stay with the process, it works, which is one of the reasons why students in my academy call the training they do "life-changing". It may feel uncomfortable at times: recognizing this and being OK with it will help you stay on track.

Resistance and what it means

Resistance is that feeling when you avoid doing something or it feels "hard". If you think back to the brain's organizing principle (see page xiii), we move away from things we perceive as threats and towards those that we see as rewards. The **amygdala** is an almond-shaped area of the brain which is responsible for deciding if something is a threat or a reward. When you're feeling resistance, it may activate the amygdala as it's sensing there is a perceived threat. This in turn activates your nervous system and can put you into fight, flight, freeze or fawn response, impacting your behaviour. This can feel like physical discomfort and you may feel fearful, scared or resentful, leading you to procrastinate, stop doing the exercise, distract yourself, over-think or obsess about the right "answer".

NERVOUS SYSTEM RESPONSES

- Flight: this is where you flee or withdraw from the perceived threat.
- Fight: this is where you face the perceived threat with aggression.
- Freeze: this is where you are immobile and unable to move when facing the threat.
- Fawn: this is where you respond to the immediate threat by wanting to please and reduce conflict.

When you do something new the **prefrontal cortex** in the brain, which is responsible for executive functions like memory, decision-making, learning and problem-solving, needs to work harder. It only has a limited capacity and uses a large amount of energy, which means it can fatigue easily. It is the reason why doing the work can feel cognitively hard: your brain is using a lot of its battery power, so do the exercises at your own pace.

Finally, your behaviour is pre-programmed in the **basal ganglia** area of your brain. This determines your thoughts, actions and assumptions. By doing these activities you are challenging the status quo and, over time, will be re-wiring this programming via neuroplasticity.

Recognize that these feelings of resistance are a psychological reaction to change. Focusing on how you will feel afterwards can help you focus on perceived pleasure, which helps tap into your dopamine response (see page xv). Simply put, imagining the benefits from completing the exercises can help you to overcome the resistance.

You will be doing "the work" yourself as your own coach through the lens of neuroscience, positive psychology and psychodynamics. This lens will help you recognize your own uniqueness and understand yourself on a deeper level.

The big questions that you will address in Step One are:

- **What does your life currently look like?** The Wheel of Life tool is the easiest way to assess this. It is a good starting point for deeper reflection and analysis, including journalling and exploring your emotional responses.
- **What are you thinking and feeling?** You will be exploring your internal world – your thoughts and emotions – so you can start to recognize patterns and connect with what is going on for you.
- **Who are you?** By looking at your personality preferences, strengths and values, you will understand more about your preferred ways of interacting with people and situations.

With this self-awareness, you will gain insight into where you want to make changes. I recommend making notes as you use the book to give yourself time to reflect on the learning from the tools and techniques.

STEP ONE AIMS

- Explore what your life looks like right now.
- Understand your thought patterns.
- Develop your connection to your emotions.
- Reflect on your personality preferences, strengths and values.
- Gain clarity on your current reality.

1

What is Your Current Reality?

I encourage you to be brave and honest to gain real clarity on the parts of your life you want to change. Although this may be challenging, hold onto the belief that this work is going to pay dividends in the long-term and that with a growth mindset you can change any aspect of your life. Remember that when you work with your brain's organizing principle toward the positive and pleasure, you open up the thinking and decision-making area in the prefrontal cortex of the brain, which in turn supports your growth. I am going to help guide you to hang out there as much as possible.

In this chapter you will explore:

- What all areas of your life currently look like
- Your thoughts and thinking patterns
- Doing a personal life audit
- Starting to build a reflective practice

What does your life currently look like?

Assessing what is going on for you right now is about painting a picture of your current situation: what your life looks and feels like, what you think about it and your behaviour.

7

Wheel of Life

A great starting point is the Wheel of Life coaching tool, which enables you to take a snapshot of where you are in all aspects of your life. I often use it at the beginning of a coaching relationship to help clients gain clarity on what is important to them and to connect with how they are thinking and feeling about each area of their life.

It enables you to reflect on where you currently are in all aspects of your life, notice what areas you may need to focus on, and check in with any resistance you have around those areas. For example, if you feel that you are "stuck" with your work-life balance, doing the Wheel of Life exercise will help you identify areas to focus on and actions you can take.

This tool was developed by Paul J Meyer, founder of the Success Motivation Institute in the 1960s. I took inspiration from the original to create my own version. I encourage my clients choose their own headings for the wheel, so it feels more personalized. If they are feeling stuck, I also offer some suggestions as a starting point.

1. Draw a large circle on a blank piece of paper.
2. Divide the circle into eight equal segments.
3. Consider the eight areas that are most important in your life right now:
   these might include *work/career, money, family, romantic relationships, friends, health/wellbeing, religion, charitable work/volunteering, spirituality, personal development, leisure/fun, work/life balance or any others of your choosing.*
4. Write the areas you have chosen as headings at the top of each segment.

5. Now, imagine you were exactly where you wanted to be in each one e.g., your career is exactly where you want it to be; you have a job that you feel valued in and you are achieving the level of success that you want. You get up for work each morning and feel energized and you know you are doing the right thing in life – this is your 10/10.

6. For each area write down what a 10/10 looks like and feels like.

7. Then, look at each segment and consider where you are right now on a scale of 0–10, with 0 being in the centre of the circle and 10 being on the outside. You can write down any notes to help you. Once you have decided, make a dot in that segment.

8. When you have marked each segment, join up the dots. Most people are not left with a circle – if you could drive a car with the wheel you have created you are more balanced than anyone else I have ever met!

REFLECTION

By doing the Wheel of Life exercise, I discovered:
- I felt resistance around …
- I found it easy to …
- I was surprised by …
- I am feeling good about these aspects of my life …
- I feel these areas could do with some work …
- The area that I would like to focus on first is …
- My preferred outcome would be …
- The first step I can take is …

Journalling

Journalling is an effective way to reflect on your thoughts and feelings. When I am feeling "stuck" in my life and business, I find that journalling helps me to make sense of what is going on, gives me clarity and reduces my stress levels. As a result, I can think more effectively and make decisions.

There are a number of ways you can journal:

- Prompted journalling
- Free writing/brain dumping/expressive writing

One of the most effective for processing emotions is free writing, where you write without prompts. To get to the stage where you are able to do this, you may find it easier to start with prompts or reflections, which you'll be doing as you work through the exercises. This is still effective as you are processing your thoughts and emotions in the same way.

I will be sharing prompts with you to structure your journalling, alongside encouraging you to practise free writing. It is about finding the approach that works best for you.

You can write in a journal or use a computer. My preference is to physically write in a journal in a room in the house where I don't work. When I am in my office it is a "work environment" and it can make me feel more stressed (especially if I have deadlines to meet). I find that physically going to a different part of the house and sitting with my journal and a pen helps me to reduce my stress levels.

If you struggle with a written journal, try recording voice notes or simply reflecting in your head. The next step would be to try to put those thoughts down on paper.

I used to resist journalling because I was afraid of what would happen when I started writing, uncertain of what thoughts and feelings might emerge. I started by buying a journal (a simple first step) and then dedicated time each week to write: at the beginning it was just a jumble of words, then over time it started to make more sense. Now, when I journal, it always feels like a release. I compare it to running: the actual experience may not be that pleasurable, but the end result is worth it.

When you start journalling think of it like a brain dump: an opportunity to get all the stuff in your head out so you can get some clarity. I liken it to the brain having plates and plates of spaghetti and, by journalling, you start to pull out the strands and unravel them. Your goal is not to have perfect strands; it's about starting to understand how they connect and link up to each other.

You are going to be doing a fair bit of reflecting throughout the book, and to get the most out of it I encourage you to be actively involved in the process. Journalling is one way of "doing" rather than just reading. When you take action, you start to build the blocks of behavioural change through neuroplasticity.

How does journalling work?

Psychologists at the University of California, Los Angeles (UCLA) studied the brains of people speaking about or writing down their emotions: when they were able to put words to the emotions the activity in the "threat" centre of the brain decreased and the activity in the ventrolateral prefrontal cortex increased. This supports the idea that talking or writing about our emotions can help us to process them, and is one reason why journalling can be so powerful, especially if you are self-coaching: effectively your journal becomes your coach.

Positive outcomes from journalling

It is this reduction in stress from the act of writing which has been shown to have cognitive and health benefits.[1] Stress and the hormones associated with it, including cortisol, can have a significant impact on your physical and emotional wellbeing. Equally, stress and cortisol impact your executive function, which reduces your ability to think clearly and make decisions, which is why an outcome from journalling is often clarity.

Writing about what you are experiencing, feeling and thinking can help you accept where you are and what has happened, and as a result you are able to move forward. It is the separation between you and your thoughts – cognitive diffusion – that helps you to observe your thoughts rather than experience them.[2]

The brain works toward anticipated pleasure and away from anticipated pain (see page xiii). If you start to build a connection in your brain between the positive feelings associated with journalling and the practice, then you are reprogramming your brain to link journalling to pleasure and you are therefore more likely to do it! This is the foundation of neuroplasticity and behavioural change.

Prompted journalling

Get out a notebook or, if you prefer working on screen, open a new document on your laptop and start by using the prompts below.

It might be that you start with five minutes and build up your practice. Remember it is when we start something new that we often feel the most resistance (see page 3).

Your brain may perceive that there will be a threat to your psychological safety if you journal. Remember to reframe!

If you find that sitting looking at the screen or journal is not working, do something to break your state. When you move your body, it can take you out of your head (we all spend far too long in our heads which ironically can stop us thinking clearly). Changing your state is a way of changing your energy and switching things up. For example, you might want to go for a walk, dance to your favourite song or do some housework and come back to the journalling afterwards.

This whole journalling process can be emotional; give yourself time and space and keep in mind that you are doing this to reduce stress and improve your physical and mental wellbeing.

You can answer all of these journalling prompts individually or choose the ones that resonate with you, and be mindful of what you're feeling when you're journalling as your emotions are also data and can give you important clues.

Home
- What does your home environment look like?
- Where do you live?
- What do you feel about where you live?
- Describe your current home.
- What do you like about your home environment?
- What don't you like about your home environment?

Wellbeing
- How would you describe your current level of health/ wellbeing?

Relationships

- How connected do you feel to others?
- What are your current relationships like?
- Describe your romantic relationships.

Family

- How would you describe your relationships with your family?

Leisure/fun

- What do you currently do for leisure/fun?
- How do you relax?

Work

- What do you do for work?
- What does your day-to-day working life look like?
- How would you describe your working relationships?

Money

- What is your current financial situation?

General life

- How would you describe your life?
- What does your day-to-day life look like?

Free writing

Rather than having set prompts or questions, free writing – or brain dumping – is a different approach to journalling. You simply open up the page and start writing, perhaps focusing on how you are feeling at that moment, what you can see around you or your thoughts.

Write the first thing that comes into your head, so be led by your intuition: it doesn't matter if it is a stream of consciousness or that it is jumbled. The aim is to make the unconscious conscious and bring it to life. Allowing the words to flow onto the page can be incredibly cathartic, so don't be surprised if you start to feel some different emotions.

Some of my clients like to do a brain dump before we start our coaching sessions as it allows them to get everything "out" and then they can come to the sessions focused. It is a strategy I use when people I work with have a lot of things going on – for example, they may be managing a team, have caring responsibilities at home or have health issues. Brain dumping helps them to process their emotions and then gain focus.

Free writing first thing in the morning before you've looked at your phone, gone on social media or watched the news means you're likely to be clearer on what you're thinking and feeling internally rather than being influenced.

Mind maps

Mind mapping is another method of becoming conscious of the unconscious – it's a term coined by psychologist Tony Buzan in the 1980s, who has gone on to publish over 100 books and has conducted considerable research into using mind maps. He found evidence that they can help you to plan and organize your thinking. The maps support the memory by "chunking" information into different sections, and encourage creative thinking – they visually allow the brain to see different opportunities, thereby opening up possibilities.

How to construct a mind map

This exploratory exercise helps you to identify your thinking and emotional response to different areas of your life. You may want to revisit the prompted journalling or free writing (see page 10) after doing this exercise to explore your thoughts and feelings at a deeper level.

1. Write your name in the centre of a blank piece of paper.
2. Draw "branches" from the centre to each area of your life e.g. your career, your relationships, your health and wellbeing. (You can use the categores from the Wheel of Life.)
3. Each branch is then split into smaller branches which relate to the main theme. e.g. relationships may have smaller branches coming off with:
   a. Positive friendships
   b. Neglected friendships
   c. New friendships you want to nurture
   d. Romantic relationships
   This is only for you, so feel free to write down people's names – you may even want to give smiley faces for where things are good, neutral faces for where they are okay and sad faces for where things aren't good.
4. You can keep adding to the map – you might want to use images or colours as well to make it more vibrant.

Here is an example:

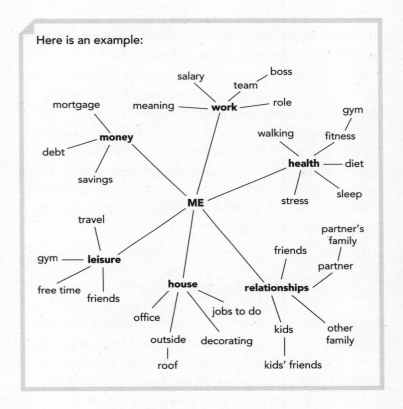

Classification systems

A final option or alternative perspective is using a classification system. If you have done the Wheel of Life exercise (see page 8), you can start by using the same categories and investigating each one – looking at what you like, what you are indifferent to and what you dislike or are unhappy with. See the exercise overleaf for an example.

This classification system can help you to get clarity, so it's important to be honest with yourself. There is no judgement from anyone, other than you, about what you put where.

The aim is to form a clearer image of how you really feel about your life right now, so that you can make changes. You don't need to fill every box for each area of your life and it may be that you choose to focus on one area specifically, if this is coming out as more important to you.

When you are doing the exercise, check in with how you are feeling; noticing your energy and emotional response can give you clues, especially as you are choosing where you put things according to how they make you feel. It can also be useful to check in with what is going on in your body as we tend to store emotions in different areas.

Classification exercise

Create a simple table with three columns, as shown opposite. Remember your choice of where you start can be influenced by what you feel is most important for you (go back to the Wheel of Life exercise and the subsequent journalling and/ or mind mapping if you have done those). Be led by what you felt when you did those exercises and remember this is only for you, so don't edit yourself. The best self-awareness comes when you can answer the questions based on your true emotional response.

I do this exercise with my team every quarter as it helps us to look at any gaps within the business and ensure that people are spending more time on what they like doing and less on what they dislike. If there is an imbalance, we can use that to look at additional resources and consider if the job roles are right for the teams' needs and our customers' needs. See the example below.

What do I like?	What don't I mind?	What do I dislike?
Home: I like where I live. It is next to a beautiful forest and there is lots of light and space.	Home: I don't mind the layout of my house.	Home: my neighbours who play really loud music. How much I feel I always need to clean.
		Fun and leisure: I haven't done anything new and different for a while. I want to be more adventurous.
	Fitness/health: I feel like I am in reasonable shape.	

REFLECTION

When you have completed the exercise, start to check in with yourself energetically and emotionally, paying attention to your feelings using the following questions:

- When you read back what you have written, how does it feel?
- What does your body feel like? Is there resistance anywhere and, if there is, what does that feel like?
- What insights have you gained from doing this exercise?

Tapping into our energy

The questions in the reflection above come from my training in energetic and somatic coaching. We can often hold insight within our bodies and our chakras, so tapping into this can give us some answers. It's always useful to feel into your body and know what is going on for you – for example, when I am stressed, I often have a knotty feeling in my left shoulder. By understanding how we feel, we can then start to recognise different types of energy – for example, the areas where we feel enthused and excited signal positive energy; the areas where we feel sadness, resentment or anger signal negative energy. We can use our energetic feelings as a compass to help us become clearer on what is going on for us and how we feel.

The more that you can be honest about what emotions and feelings are coming up for you, the more you can then change your reality. This isn't about suddenly throwing out everything in your life, although it may mean making a significant change.

Repressed emotions

Any physical discomfort you feel in your body may link back to repressed emotions. For example, maybe you have been holding emotion such as resentment or grief, which has then shown up as a back problem. Psychiatrist Dr Srini Pillay has suggested that those suffering from catastrophic thinking – where we allow our thoughts to spiral to a worst-case scenario – are more likely to experience chronic back pain.[3]

There is some evidence that we "hold" onto our repressed emotions and these can cause us illness in the future. In Traditional Chinese Medicine (TCM) the belief is that certain emotions are linked to different body parts, for example anger is linked to the liver.

The chakras

Chakras form the basis of a lot of energetic work and originated in India around 1,000 BC. If you are familiar with yoga, meditation or reiki, you will notice how they reference the chakras.

Chakras are energy centres in our body. There are seven main chakras which run down your spine, extending from the base of your spine to the crown of your head: root, sacral, solar plexus, heart, throat, third eye and crown. When our chakras are open or balanced, we are in harmony. If they are overactive or underactive, it can impact our health and wellbeing and manifest in physical and emotional symptoms – for example, if your root chakra is blocked, it can cause anxiety or depression.

During my training as a Spiral Energy Practitioner, we explored the emotions connected with each chakra and the areas in the body that were connected to these. When I work with clients,

I support them to help clear the emotions they are holding onto in each of their chakras.

These ancient philosophies make the mind-body connection explicit. I would always urge caution around illness and disease as, although there may be a link to our emotions and repressed emotions, it is not helpful to suggest causation or attribute blame.

My sliding doors moment happened when I was at my worst … In September 2013, after a friend's wedding, I woke up with a banging hangover. I had behaved like a bit of a (a lot of a) d*ck and felt awful, spending the morning wallowing in self-pity. It was the wake-up call I needed (huge apologies to my friends for their wedding day being impacted in order for me to get that reality check). I realized that I could spend my time getting drunk and doing everything I could to forget how unhappy I was or I could do something about it.

I drank too much because I didn't feel good. The link between drinking and feeling good is well-documented: in the short term you get Dutch courage and confidence so you feel better, then you cross the line and you look and are a mess (and wake up with guilt and regret). I had crossed that line many times. I ended up behaving in ways I never would normally, and when the alcohol-induced anxiety had lifted it made me reflect on what I wanted.

On that day I finally committed to being honest about where I was in my life: I had a good job and my own flat, but I was in debt and miserable. I decided to make some pretty dramatic changes by cutting down on booze, doing more yoga and making a commitment to actively date. By Christmas

2013 I had met the man who is now my husband and was fitter and happier than I had been in years.

I had to start by examining my life, identifying what I wanted to change and going for it. It started small with some journalling, re-visiting CBT (Cognitive Behavioural Therapy) sessions and signing up to a mindfulness course. By 2014 I was studying coaching and NLP, and had upped my leadership coaching alongside my senior leadership role.

Since this point, my self-development journey has accelerated and now personal development is the cornerstone of my life and business. I am by no means "fixed" and by no means perfect. I'm sure when I write a book ten years from now my wisdom will be greater, but right now I can share how ten years of work has helped me transform and access over 28 years of study in the psychology/neuroscience field. Lots of this wasn't new to me; I just hadn't done much with it before.

You don't need to be at that low point to move forward. I share this example because it shows that even when we are feeling at our worst, we can make a positive change and sometimes we need that reality check.

Finding your focus

I hope that by doing the exercises so far you are much clearer about what your life looks and feels like right now. Throughout the next section, you will be engaging with your current reality and building self-awareness.

When people come for coaching, they often have a particular goal or area of focus in mind, however, it is usually more complex than they originally think. They may be looking at what is above the iceberg (see page 2). The reality is it is often the things underneath, such as beliefs, values and thoughts, which underpin lasting behavioural change. The process of coaching or self-coaching makes the unconscious conscious, which is the first step of the change process.

The areas you assessed in the Wheel of Life exercise (see page 8) are interlinked and if you are struggling in one area, it is likely to affect other areas too. Our brains are made up of millions of neurons working together to build neural pathways. These work to build the blueprint for how we are and how we respond to things across all areas of our lives. Cognitively, we only have so much bandwidth and if it is being used, for example, on our relationship or our work, it will impact other areas of our lives. When you attempt to put something in a box and not deal with it, your brain still knows it is there and it will use up some of the bandwidth that you have.

That is why, even though you may have already chosen a focus for this book, I encourage you to keep an open mind; as you start to build your self-awareness, you may realize that there are other things which you need to explore and coach yourself through. By spending time digging into each area of your life, you can paint a picture of how things are. Remember, this is your starting point. If you revisit these exercises a few months from now, and you have been taking action, you will have a very different reality. That is why I love personal development and self-coaching – we can make change!

Barriers to change

It is important that any work we do is contextualized – for example, my husband's experience as a black man is very different to mine as a white woman. My experience growing up in a white middle-class background is different to those who have had more disadvantaged upbringings. Let's be honest about these differences now and acknowledge your experiences and the inheritance of your ancestors' experiences and belief structures.

We know that some people have more privilege and opportunities than others – for example, white, heterosexual males who went to private school and/or Oxbridge have an advantage when it comes to politics (especially traditionally and in the Conservative Party). They have more opportunity.

Our level of privilege can be impacted by our age, social class, ethnicity, wealth, sexual orientation, gender, gender identity, nationality, neurology, disability, physical attractiveness or geographical location.

My clients have come from all over the world and have had a whole host of backgrounds and experiences. Although change is always possible, it is important to be aware that for some people change is harder.

What does your day-to-day look like?

You have looked at the big picture, now let's get into the detail. How often do you look at your day-to-day reality and explore what that looks like?

The final exercise for this chapter is to keep a diary so you can explore what is happening each day. Do this for a week – choose a typical week, rather than when you are on holiday or away for work. Gradually, you will start to build a picture of your day-to-day life. This is a useful way to reflect on your emotions and thoughts, as well as what you are doing and your context and environment. If you don't want to write a diary, you can record voice notes instead.

A simple way to start is at the end of the day answer the following questions:

- What did I do?
- Where was I?
- How did I feel?
- Who did I see?
- What do I recall thinking?
- What was good?
- What didn't work out?
- How do I feel about the day?

By checking in with yourself every day, you are giving yourself space to explore on a deeper level and holding up a mirror to what is really going on. This may be hard and you may want to put the book down now or file it away for "another day". If you need to, feel free to come back to this when you feel stronger and more focused.

KEY POINTS TO REMEMBER

- The Wheel of Life and Mind Mapping exercises will help you identify your current reality and what is going on in different areas of your life.
- Journalling is a great tool for gaining clarity and improving wellbeing.
- You can't change what you don't measure – you need to do this "life audit" to move forward and revisit it to see the progress you have made.
- Your context and environment are important – you can change these over time too.
- Stay open-minded as you work out what you want to focus on first.
- You can gain more self-awareness by keeping a diary of your day-to-day reality.

2

What is Going on in
Your Inner World?

We've looked at your outer world, so now let's dive into your inner world. Personal development is an inside job as you work on your thoughts, emotions and feelings. In this chapter you're going to be going deeper underneath that iceberg, into the unconscious and making sense of what is going on for you cognitively and emotionally. By doing so, you can act on the parts you can control to move forward. The brain is where change takes place, so you need to know what's happening there!

In this chapter you will explore:

- Your thoughts
- Your inner critic and how it keeps you small
- Your emotions and how you feel

Your inner critic and emotions impact how you perceive your current reality and what you think is possible for you. Addressing your thoughts is the first step to creating new behaviours and building new neural pathways – our thoughts can equally keep us stuck in unhelpful patterns and situations. That is why you will explore them now as a way of transforming yourself from the inside out.

You will notice that after each exercise I ask you to consider how you are thinking and feeling, as thoughts and emotions are clues which can help with the quest for clarity. You are being a detective in your own life.

You'll be exploring your "shadow" and the work of Carl Jung later in the book (see page 49) to build on what you have done in this section. For now, this is about you realizing that feeling good doesn't need to be about everything being perfect. This is about you celebrating who you are right now with every dimension of you and your being.

Understanding your thoughts

One of the best ways to start when exploring your unconscious is to address that inner dialogue and how you speak to yourself on a day-to-day basis. The most consistent voice is that inner critic or inner cheerleader. A huge part of the work that I do as a coach is supporting my clients to make sense of their thoughts and I do this in various ways:

- Asking questions and acting as a mirror to reflect back
- Exploring the language and words they use
- Being explicit with questioning around what they are thinking
- Getting them to reflect on what they are thinking

Through listening and questioning, I help my clients make the unconscious conscious. You are going to be taking on this role when you self-coach, which is why there are lots of prompts throughout the book to help you reflect and ask yourself questions. In coaching lingo I talk about "holding space" for my clients: you can apply this to yourself by giving yourself time to think, so do take the time you need to answer these questions effectively.

Every day I spend time reflecting on my thinking. It might be that I have felt upset about something or that I am finding something challenging and questioning my ability. By allowing myself to listen to what I am saying to myself, I can change that dialogue – for example, when I am struggling with a task and telling myself that I am useless and I can't do it, I remind myself that I believe in growth mindset and I can improve! Knowing that my brain is doing its best to keep me safe helps here too. By being able to reframe my thinking, I'm able to feel happier and more confident in every situation and it's as simple as building a new practice, which you repeat to embed it in your brain through neuroplasticity.

Now, let's look at your thoughts and that internal dialogue. A great way to track what you say to yourself is to keep a "thought diary", which could be part of your daily diary. This will help you to start seeing patterns and gain clarity.

Keeping a thought diary

Your task is to write down the significant and repetitive thoughts that you are having over a 72-hour period. Make a note of key words or phrases that you tell yourself. Use something that is relatively portable, such as your phone or a notepad and pen, as you will need to jot your thoughts down regularly.

At the end of each day and again at the end of the 72-hour period, reflect on the following questions:

- What repetitive thoughts am I having?
- Which of these are the most damaging?
- What do these thoughts stop me doing?

By identifying our thoughts, we can change them. This exercise can be triggering, so remember to treat yourself with compassion.

Challenging your thoughts

When you have been able to "catch" your thoughts, you can start to process them and look at alternatives as a way of reframing them from unhelpful to helpful thoughts.

A great starting point is to ask yourself these questions:

- How valid is this thought?
- What is an alternative, more helpful thought?
- How can I think differently about this?

For example: if your thought is that you are not experienced enough to ask for a promotion, you may reflect by asking:

- How valid is this thought? When you consider the evidence, are you really not experienced enough or do you have examples of others with a similar level of experience who have been promoted?
- What is an alternative, more helpful thought? In this example, it might be "I am building up my experience so I can get promoted and further my career."

- How can I think differently about this? You could look at all the skills you already have and see this as a stepping stone to the next level.

When you reset the unhelpful thinking model, you consciously acknowledge the thought – you might even want to say hello to it – and then say something like "You are not helpful". After this, consider what a more helpful thought could be as a reframe.

Some of your unhelpful and negative thoughts may be from your current contexts and situations, as well as your emotions. Often, you create a false reality of a situation in your head based on your perceptions. Your negative thought patterns can escalate if you're unhappy in another part of your life and you can project this onto other people or other situations – for example, if you are struggling at work and have a negative relationship with your boss, it can impact your personal relationships at home.

Being able to look at your thoughts and reflect on what is true/real and what isn't is a brilliant first step, as you can sometimes easily see how you have gotten into a negative thought cycle. A great example is when you message a friend and they don't reply. These are some different scenarios that you might come up with:

Scenario one: You assume they are busy and will reply when they get a chance. You don't read into it and you don't give it anymore thought.

Scenario two: You start to look for reasons, thinking that maybe they don't like you anymore. You think back to when you last saw them and wonder if you did anything that may have upset them. You start to create a story in your head where you have upset them and they don't want to hang out with you anymore. You start to feel anxious about what you might have done and find it difficult to focus on anything else.

** Disclaimer: I don't really drink much anymore as that all-consuming anxiety and fear is too much; I am always convinced I have upset everyone. Once, I really did upset a friend with a "joke" that I made about his boyfriend which was obviously not funny. It was about 20 years ago now, but I don't think it has helped my alcohol anxiety!

Scenario three: You look at your previous text messages from your friend. You realize that you didn't reply to their last message and haven't been that good at replying or keeping in touch. You drop them a follow-up voice note explaining how you have had a lot on and been a bit flaky, and would love to catch up. You feel happy to have been honest and taken responsibility to rebuild the relationship.

** Disclaimer: Again, this is me! I often tend to reply to messages in my head only. Luckily my friends all know this about me!

Now, it could be that you have upset your friend and they are ghosting you, although that is probably unlikely. What you are doing in scenario two is catastrophizing, which means you are imagining the worst-case scenario. When you do this, you're making other people's behaviour about you, not them, and creating stories that support these assumptions. Being able to take a step back from what is going on and look at other scenarios can help you recognize this pattern and calm your nervous system, so you can park these feelings. Always assuming the worst uses up a lot of nervous energy and takes you away from focusing on what is important.

Understanding different perceptions and perspectives

Your unique experience and the lens with which you view situations impacts your perception of them and what information you think is more or less important. Everyone brings their own perspective based on their context, experience, personality, preferences, values and belief structure. Learning to accept that people perceive things differently can be transformational as it gives you more perspective. You can expend so much energy persuading others that you're "right". If you let go of this, you are much more likely to feel content and have that "inner peace" yogis always talk about.

In a world which is defined by what is right and wrong, looking at the greyness in-between helps us to appreciate others and means we can step away from judgement and step into compassion – for example, you may get removed from a group WhatsApp chat as you can no longer make an event. You told the host that you were suffering with your mental health which is why you couldn't come. You might see the person as being rude and uncaring as they removed you and didn't check in, while they see themselves as having done you a favour so you aren't inundated with updates and plan to catch up with you later. The meaning you attach is based on your viewpoint and experience as well as how you're feeling at the time.

A valuable way to start considering different perspectives is to reflect on the following questions:

- What other ways could people interpret this situation?
- How might the people involved see it differently?
- What else could be impacting their behaviour?
- How much of this is really about me?

I have been in many situations where I thought people were either being mean to me on purpose or talking about me, and in the majority of cases I was wrong. I have also been through experiences with people where we have felt completely differently about what happened afterwards. Often, we make things about us because we spend the majority of our time in our own head, which massively impacts how we show up and perceive things.

The inner critic

Our inner critic is that unhelpful voice that most of us have in our heads, stopping us from doing things; it says you are too old/young/fat/thin/stupid or you aren't clever/young/experienced/good enough – you know the drill. This voice is there to keep you safe. In fact, from an evolutionary perspective, this is the role of the brain. The amygdala is the key part of the brain looking out for perceived and anticipated threats or rewards, which works well in some situations – for example, you hear a loud noise, your brain signals danger and you run away. Our inner critic can also keep us safe in the same way if it perceives we may be putting ourselves in psychological danger by stepping out of our comfort zone – for example, if you ask someone out on a date, you might be rejected, which is a threat, therefore you avoid doing it. You tell yourself a whole host of reasons as to why you will be rejected, which can then feed into a cycle of self-criticism.

When you see your inner critic as a way of your ego staying safe by avoiding the possibility of failure or rejection, you can understand it.

Changing your thought diet

Negative thoughts only disappear through self-awareness. When you have identified those story loops, which you play on repeat (a bit like *Friends* in the 2000s on E4), you have to take action to change them. Like a weed, it isn't about pulling off the top part; it is about going down to the root and putting in the effort there.

According to a study by Tseng and Poppenk in 2020[4], the average person has about 6,000 thoughts a day: this is a considerable chunk of thinking that you do daily. Some thoughts may be automatic: "I'm hungry", "I feel cold", "I'm tired"; others might be much more complex, such as "Will I be able to do this effectively?", "What does the success or failure of this project mean for me?"

Earlier on in the chapter (see page 30), you were encouraged to keep a thought diary (this is a gentle nudge to get it done if you haven't already). It's important to do this as it can help you spot your most prevalent thoughts.

After identifying those thoughts, it is worth digging deeper by answering these questions which can be used as journalling prompts:

- Where does this thought come from?
- How is it helping me?
- What do I need to believe to have an alternative way of thinking?
- Who would I need to be to think in this way?
- What is an alternative thought?
- How can I create evidence to support this new thought?
- How do I need to be to support this new thought?

You can re-wire your neural pathways, starting with your thoughts, through neuroplasticity and this is often the first stage of behavioural change. By changing your thoughts over time, you can change your thinking. And thinking alone can be sufficient (although I do believe you need to back it up with action). In 2004, researchers at Cleveland University found that when they imagined doing bicep curls five times a week for six weeks, they had a 10.8 per cent increase in muscle strength[5]. We can really think ourselves stronger!

This is your first step in feeling better: uncovering what is not helping you internally and starting to take positive steps to change. When you acknowledge that you can't change the past and that many of those voices in your head which are telling you to do or not do things are not even real (and may not even be your voice) everything changes. You begin to let go of the past iteration of you, and allow yourself to embrace the new version.

I've had my fair share of negative thoughts in life and been plagued by my inner critic, so I appreciate how hard it can be to get out of these patterns of thinking. When I was 18, the week before my A-levels started, I was in a car accident and a close friend died. I was driving and therefore I lived with survivor guilt and PTSD for many years. I remember, about nine months after the accident, feeling like I couldn't even get out of bed to go to the toilet because I felt so worthless. I didn't share this feeling with anyone as I was so ashamed about not being OK, and I didn't want to worry my mum and dad. To the outside world, despite the accident, I had passed my A-levels with flying colours and was taking a gap year, working in a local call centre before I went (ran away) to Australia.

Alongside the grief and the guilt, I had this overwhelming feeling that I needed to get on with my life and do something because I had not been injured. In a way, that responsibility was a positive and a negative as it spurred me not to sit and wallow (which, to be honest, was what I wanted to do most days). It also acted like another weight around my neck as I realized that I was merely going through the motions most days rather than really living my life.

I felt like no one would want to be around me, and I remember being bullied and insulted consistently throughout my teens. I felt worthless and being told you are worthless, even if it is from an overweight guy who has significant mental health issues, you feel it even more.

*I remember having some counselling sessions. The counsellor said to me "You will never get over this and it will define your life". That was a f*ck you moment for sure. I knew that I wouldn't let this define my life, I knew that despite everything that I felt I still had a choice. (Note: this was an unskilled counsellor, who didn't have the ability to hold and support me with the trauma and doesn't represent all the brilliant counsellors and therapists there are in the world.)*

Overcoming something that is so traumatic, especially when you feel guilt and responsibility for the trauma, is not easy. I believed running away to Australia would help me distance myself from what had happened, but everywhere I went I seemed to meet people from my town, which only served to remind me that I couldn't get away unless I dealt with it in my head.

Even before I was 18, I had been reading psychology books and applied to study it at university. I wanted to know what was wrong with me and why I was different. Before the accident,

I was probably suffering from mild depression and I wasn't confident within myself. If anything, the accident intensified those feelings and gave me even more of a reason to want to understand myself.

Through a BA and MA in Psychology (with Management and Education), I learned more about the human mind. I ran the Psychological Society and was exposed to things like hypnosis back in the late 1990s when most people thought it was an intervention that would make you bark like a dog!

Over the years, I started to have my own interventions: I went back to counselling, especially when I got into a lot of debt in my first year of university (I learnt this was a coping mechanism as I was so desperate to fit in). I had spent a fortune on clothes and would always be the first to buy drinks for others because I wanted them to like me. It is a fairly typical story that sometimes we think we are so worthless that we have to pay people to be our friends, and this is genuinely how I felt.

Underneath it all I didn't love myself or even like myself very much. I worked with a CBT therapist, I had hypnosis, I worked with coaches and mentors, and did a whole array of courses. I am not suggesting you have to do any of these (and indeed in this book I share my biggest learnings so you don't have to spend what I spent!). For me, it was the journey and the path that I needed to go on.

That day in 1996 was pivotal to my life. It is not an experience I often talk about, although now the aftermath is what has enabled me to really connect with others and to understand about our brains and how we can all, whatever has happened to us, move forward and change our lives (and it is not always easy – I mean is it ever?).

Your emotions and feelings

Alongside your thoughts sit your emotions. In fact, they impact each other:

- For example, say you have a bad night's sleep. Maybe you were woken up by foxes outside or noisy neighbours. You wake up cranky and in a bad mood. This mood then impacts what you are thinking. Thinking in a negative way impacts your mood further. And so it continues in a cycle.
- Conversely, if you are with people you love and who make you feel good, you are much more likely to think positively. This makes you feel good and the cycle continues.

Our thoughts don't operate in a vacuum. Our emotional state, environment and company all impact our thoughts. Simply thinking happy positive thoughts won't make you happy. When you increase your self-awareness and work out what impacts you, it will enable you to make changes on a deeper level.

This book is not about toxic positivity, where you say "Everything is OK, it's all fine" when really you are crumbling. We're hardwired to focus on the negative; when our brains are presented with negative stimuli we have higher levels of neural activity, meaning that we pay more attention to negative events[6]. Cognitively, they hold more interest. This may be because we are more likely to feel the stress response from negative events. This bias comes from evolution: as a species our ancestors needed to pay attention to the threats in the environment to survive. Now we know it has a negative impact on our wellbeing.

When you go to bed and think about your day, you are much more likely to think about the things that didn't go well rather than all the things that did. As a coach, I help clients to get to know their emotions, tip the balance towards experiencing more positive emotions and identify the negative in order to reframe them where appropriate or move through them. Sometimes, you need to sit in the sadness or anger to move toward the joy – it is the old adage, better out than in. If you're able to cry you are processing emotion rather than suppressing it. When you suppress emotions, you store them in your body which is likely to come back and bite you in the bum at some point!

Coaching is more than thinking; it's also about exploring, classifying and labelling feelings. Often this work can be challenging as you may not have had your feelings validated as a child; you may have learned to bury them and just get on with things. It can be difficult – give yourself some time and most of all focus on your needs and looking after yourself, practising your own self-care.

Identifying emotions

Psychologist Robert Plutnik suggests that we have eight core emotions: anger, fear, sadness, disgust, surprise, anticipation, trust and joy. In this exercise, you explore and identify emotions, reflecting on what each one feels like to you, and what is going on in both your body and energetically when you feel each one. This is part of the work I do as an energy practitioner, supporting people in exploring how their emotions manifest in their body and their memories. The more that you're able to recognize your thoughts and feelings and start to look at what may be behind them, the more you can change. Remember to give yourself time and space when you work through this exercise.

For each of the eight core emotions, complete the sentences. Here's an example:

When I feel angry ...
I also feel cross, fearful, sad and tetchy. I know I am angry because I start to get really irritable. I feel like my face gets flushed and I can often feel my fists clenching. There is a tightness in my body and I have this overwhelming desire to shout. I feel like I don't have my normal control and it feels physical rather than cognitive.

When I feel angry ...
I also feel ...
I know I am angry because ...
I feel it in my body by ...
Anything else (e.g. thoughts – what you are/aren't doing) ...

When I feel fear ...
I also feel ...
I know I am fearful because ...
I feel it in my body by ...
Anything else (e.g. thoughts – what you are/aren't doing) ...

When I feel sadness ...
I also feel ...
I know I am sad because ...
I feel it in my body by ...
Anything else (e.g. thoughts – what you are/aren't doing) ...

When I feel disgust ...
I also feel ...
I know I am disgusted because ...

I feel it in my body by ...
Anything else (e.g. thoughts – what you are/aren't doing) ...

When I feel surprise ...
I also feel ...
I know I am surprised because ...
I feel it in my body by ...
Anything else (e.g. thoughts – what you are/aren't doing) ...

When I feel anticipation ...
I also feel ...
I know I am feeling anticipation because ...
I feel it in my body by ...
Anything else (e.g. thoughts – what you are/aren't doing) ...

When I feel trust ...
I also feel ...
I know I trust because ...
I feel it in my body by ...
Anything else (e.g. thoughts – what you are/aren't doing) ...

When I feel joy ...
I also feel ...
I know I am feeling joy because ...
I feel it in my body by ...
Anything else (e.g. thoughts – what you are/aren't doing) ...

I always support my clients to explore their learning from doing this exercise. Often this goes beyond the exercise itself and it is always useful to reflect on how you feel and what you're thinking during the exercise.

REFLECTION

You may want to journal your responses to the following questions:

- What did you learn from doing this exercise?
- What will you do differently as a result of doing it?
- How did you feel about it?
- What were you thinking?
- Where did you feel resistance?

Tracking emotions

In a similar vein to how you looked at your thoughts, you can also track your emotions. The premise of this is to start to see patterns (you may also start to notice connections between your thoughts and feelings). Consider also how often you are honest with people about how you are feeling. This doesn't need to be a discussion about your innermost feelings with all and sundry, but it is about allowing yourself to feel, and express those feelings, rather than putting on a brave face.

Keep your journal with you, whether it be physical or digital, to track your emotions and how you're feeling. You may want to consider the following questions:

- What emotions have you felt?
- What happened to make you feel these emotions – situations/events/people?
- What was your physical response?

Good questions to ask yourself at the end of the day in your journalling practice are "How am I feeling?", "What do I need?",

"What made me respond in that way?". Remember your emotional response is often instinctive, but learning to spot clues and cues can change our responses.

For example, if I'm feeling lonely and disconnected, I check in with why and what has happened that day. With this insight, I will then message or call a friend or arrange a coffee date or go upstairs and ask my husband when he is free for a chat. I know that I need to have some more connection to make me feel good.

With this self-awareness of your emotions and your triggers, you can start to plan – for example, if certain family members can make you feel sad or angry, think about what you can do before or after seeing them. Equally, you may want to explore why they make you feel like this.

KEY POINTS TO REMEMBER

- Recognize your unhelpful, negative thoughts and reframe them into helpful, postitive thoughts.
- Start to build more helpful ways of thinking.
- Identify how different emotions manifest in your body and where you feel them the most.
- Consider what your triggers are for various emotions and what you can do to prevent them.

3

Who Are You?

We looked at where you currently are with different areas of your life in Chapter 1 and started to look underneath the iceberg at your thoughts and emotions in Chapter 2. Now your self-exploration will go even deeper as you look at yourself through the lens of personality preferences, strengths and values. This chapter is based on positive psychology and is key to helping you understand your behaviour.

In this chapter you will explore how to:

- Identify your personality and behavioural preferences looking at DISC and JUNG-style approaches
- Step into self-acceptance and self-awareness
- Understand what your needs are and how these show up in how you behave
- Identify your driving values
- Get clear on your strengths

This is about understanding who you are and your preferences, and starting to look at how they show up in how you behave.

It is the start of radical self-awareness, which is at the heart of coaching; the more you know about yourself, the more you understand and take into your relationships and interactions.

When you connect with who you are and the way that you show up, everything changes. It is easy to say "be more you" or "just be yourself", but what if the essence of you has been hidden under "shoulds" and labels that no longer serve you, and you have been feeling uncomfortable for years?

One of the founding principles of Psychology is that everyone is a unique individual. Your personalities and preferences are unique and research has found your personality traits are relatively stable over time. I believe that a big part of this stability is due to the fact that we believe our personality is fixed or set, and those around us see us in a certain way based on their past perception and experience. Therefore, we act to type. You are able to change any element of your personality and preferences, if you have the desire and motivation to do so, however most of us don't!

I'm going to share two different approaches to looking at personality and behavioural preferences, both of which help you build a clearer picture of who you are. As a coach, I am led by my clients' own desires of what they want to explore and what they feel most drawn to: what resonates with one person may not resonate with the next.

Personality and behavioural preferences are often the easiest things for you to identify – for example, you may know if you prefer being on your own or with others. Returning to the iceberg analogy (see page 2), these are the things that you can see and feel are tangible. When you understand your preferences, it can help you to realize how you communicate and what you tend to be drawn to, which can also impact what you see as important – this then becomes useful information when you are looking at your strengths and values.

Self-awareness and identity

Who are you? It's a question you probably don't ask yourself that often. When you introduce yourself to someone new, you may "label" yourself by telling them what you do for a living, where you live and your relationship status. This is, of course, part of who you are but not the entirety. This work is about going beyond those labels. I'm not suggesting that your opening gambit becomes "I am an extrovert who gets my energy from being around others and thrives when given complex problems to solve" (although this would be an interesting thing to test out!). This is about bringing more of your whole self to your interactions and relationships.

Your brain's neural pathways predict how you behave based on how frequently you use them as they are based on association: the more that the neurons fire together, the more they wire together. Remember you can always change the wiring! This is one of the things I love about coaching; you get to see inside someone else's brain without any blood involved!

Resisting change

External stimuli, such as work pressures, looking after your family and relationships, and managing your finances, can reduce the desire for you to address your innermost thoughts and feelings. The resistance is often there because, on a subconscious level, you don't want to go there. How often do you avoid thinking about how you feel as you know if you did, you would have to do something about it? I know I spent many years in the wrong job or the wrong relationship as I felt it was easier and less painful than deciding to change. Most of us crave a simple life and when you face up to and confront your problems, you need to do something about them. Making changes is scary but it is also exciting, as you embrace what you really want and step into that new identity.

Your personality and behavioural preferences

Your behavioural and personality preferences influence how you act. Understanding these helps you to understand others and build more effective relationships because you're not only learning about your typical behaviour you're learning about other preferences so you start to recognise how behaviours are caused by these preferences. You may mask your preferences to conform to a dominant culture, both at work and in relationships. When you recognize these behaviours, you can take off that mask!

Renowned psychiatrist and psychoanalyst Carl Jung, first looked at personality over 100 years ago, coining the term "predictably different". This describes how you can classify people based on how they usually react and respond. His work led to the development of personality tests, which assess an individual's attributes. In the last 50 years, there's been an explosion in these tests, with them being used globally in businesses and as part of personal development, demonstrating the thirst we all have to understand ourselves better.

DISC

I train in DISC (Dominance, Influence, Steadiness or Compliance) profiling and have trained thousands of people to determine their preferences using these assessments. I find that DISC is a simple and straightforward way to start to understand yourself and recognize differences in your behaviour and communication preferences.

DISC is a way of classifying your preferences based on two criteria:

1. How outgoing or reserved you are. This is measured by the pace that you like to do things. Are you someone who is fast-paced? Tends to "talk to think" (rather than think before you talk) and likes to go through life quickly. Or are you slower paced, more reflective and someone who takes your time? Most of us have a natural preference. (I am fast-paced which is why this book has been a labour of love!)
2. Whether you have a preference for tasks or for people. Some people are naturally more drawn to tasks – they are goal-focused and they love working through strategy, while others are drawn to people and like to get things done through collaboration.

When you recognize your preferences, you can start to reflect on how you may be perceived by others. As someone who is fast-paced and goal-oriented, I learned early on that these were not "female" traits and I therefore masked them to "fit in". Equally, at times my directness has been mistaken for something else, which is why it is so important to consider not only how we communicate, but also who we are communicating with.

Understanding your preferences

Choose either A or B, then Y or Z for each. When you answer, imagine you are in a work situation:

A) Do you tend to make decisions quickly?
/B) Do you tend to take time to make decisions?
- A) *Do you tend to be direct in your communication?*
B) *Do you tend to be more indirect?*
A) Do you have a tendency to be future focused?
/ B) Do you tend to be more focused in the present/past?
A) *Do you tend to do things at a fast pace?*
/ B) *Do you tend to work at a slower pace?*

If you chose mainly As, you are more likely to be outgoing.
If you chose mainly Bs, you are more likely to be reserved.

Y) Do you talk more about things?
Z) Do you talk more about people?
Y) *Are you more focused on the task?*
Z) *Are you most focused on the people?*
Y) Do you tend to show less emotion than others?
Z) Do you tend to show emotion easily?
Y) *At work I like to know what is expected of me with processes and systems.*
Z) *At work I enjoy interacting with others.*

If you chose mostly Ys, you are more likely to be task-focused. If you chose mostly Zs, you are more likely to be people-focused.

Finally, look at these statements and see which are most like you:

1) When I am working with others on a problem, how am I most likely to behave?
   - I want to make a quick decision. (D)
   - I'm considering how everyone else feels. (S)
   - I'm thinking "Let's just have fun and go with the flow". (I)
   - I'm thinking "Let's consider what else is needed to make a decision, what data do we have?" (C)

2) How do I feel about detailed work, research and analysis?
   - This is my sweet spot, I love it. (C)
   - If it helps makes things easier for others, I'll do it. (S)
   - If it will help get better, quicker results, I'll do it. (D)
   - If it will help others think more of me, I'll do it. (I)

3) If I go to an event where there are lots of people I don't know, how am I most likely to behave?
   - Identify who I want to speak with before the event and speak to them. (D)
   - Seek out a small group who I may already know and chat to them. (S)
   - Embrace the opportunity to speak to as many people as possible. (I)
   - Find somewhere to sit and observe everyone. (C)

4) I would most describe myself as:
   - Direct, goal-focused, driven and motivated. (D)
   - Fun, outgoing, persuasive, creative. (I)
   - Kind, helpful, team-player, supportive. (S)
   - Accurate, logical, correct, data-driven. (C)

5) The best praise I can receive is:
- You always achieve so much. (D)
- You are appreciated and valued. (S)
- Your work is excellent and detailed. (C)
- You are fantastic and inspirational. (I)

Total D: 1
Total I: ←
Total S: 3
Total C: ↑

When you have your answers, you can see the typical preferences you have: the higher you are in each category the more likely you are to have this as a preference, the lower you are the less likely:

	People-focused	Task-focused
Outgoing	I (influence)	D (dominance)
Reserved	S (steadiness)	C (control)

This quick exercise you've just done will reveal your natural preferences. If you tend to be more outgoing and task-focused, you are a D preference – dominant, driven and goal-focused. Ds tend to be direct with their communication and are focused on getting results, they work quickly and are flexible in their approach as they are driven by success. They can be seen as rude or abrupt as they are often direct and focused on what is next, rather than checking in with people.

If you tend to be more outgoing and people-focused, you are an I preference, which is described as influence. You tend to be outgoing, lively, enthusiastic, optimistic and seen as warm and interested in people. You can be very creative with lots of ideas, although you don't always follow through with them. You like to liked and are seen as a positive influence on others.

If you tend to be more reserved and people-focused, you are a S preference, which is described as steadiness. You tend to be loyal, stable and are seen as kind. You focus on others' needs first and you are a great team player, ensuring that everyone feels OK. You don't like change so need time to adjust.

If you tend to be more reserved and task-focused, you are a C preference, which is described as compliance. You have a preference for data, analytics and doing research. You take time to make an informed decision. You tend to be focused on rigour and getting things right.

All these preferences blend together, so it is normal to see different elements of yourself in different descriptions. Equally, each of the types has its own temperature gauge, so you may be more or less than someone else with the same preference.

An alternative approach from Jung

DISC is a great starting point for looking at preferences. To help you gain awareness of your personality "type", I'm going to draw on the work of Jung.

You may be familiar with the concept of extroversion and introversion. Often extroverts are painted as loud and brash and introverts as deep thinking and reflective. Most people are neither completely one nor the other, but lie at some point along the continuum. The measure is really about where we get our energy from – introverts get their energy from being alone and need that time to recharge, while extroverts get their energy from being around others.

External circumstances can have an impact on our preferences – for example, the coronavirus pandemic in 2020/21 saw most of the world in lockdown. Many extroverts found that when they came out of the pandemic their preferences had changed and they needed more time alone, especially if they had been in busy households. Conversely, many introverts craved more human connection as they'd had their fill of "alone time".

One deciding factor in how our introversion/extroversion shows up is our context. Working from home can be great for people who have more of a preference for introversion. For those who get their energy from others, it can feel incredibly isolating. I have worked with a few clients who are high on the extroversion scale, live alone and work from home and they are miserable.

Jung developed three additional continuums which can be used to determine your preferences: on each continuum you assess where you sit and which is your more dominant preference.

Sensing vs Intuition: A preference for sensing means you pay attention to your own physical realities and the information you receive from your senses; seeing, hearing, touching, tasting and smelling. You tend to be more focused on facts and details, looking for evidence. By contrast, if you have a preference for intuition, you have a tendency to be future-focused and you're motivated by possibilities, often inferring things about events rather than being stuck in the detail.

Thinking vs Feeling: This explains how we make decisions. If you have a preference for thinking, you're often seen as logical and data-driven. You may draw up a list of the pros and cons to help you decide something. By contrast, if you have a preference for feeling, you are motivated by harmony and consider what other people are feeling and thinking when you make decisions.

Perceiving vs Judging: This is the lens through which we operate in the world. If you have a preference for perceiving, you tend to be flexible and open to external stimuli and often appear to be making decisions in the here and now. If you have a preference for judging, you're much more likely to enjoy planning and order as well as having a sense of control over what will happen in your life.

Jung's personality preferences – which one are you?

Each of us has our own unique blueprint, which is made up of our results on our four preferences. Remember, we are all on the continuums.

Under each bold heading couplet, circle what is most like you – this will give you an idea of your preferences. Consider which feels most like you and you have the strongest preference for. If you're really struggling, it may indicate that you're in the middle of the continuum. Very few people are 50/50, although many of us are 40/60, so ask yourself if you had to choose which you would typically pick.

Extroversion

Gain energy from being around others

Enjoy being in groups

Wide circle of friends / acquaintances

Introversion

Gain energy from being alone

Reflect on situations

Prefer small groups

Sensation

Focus on physical reality

Facts and details

Look for evidence

Intuition

Focus on possibilities

Future-focused

Read between the lines

Thinking

Logical decision-making

Look at pros and cons

Data driven

Feeling

Other people's viewpoints

People-based decisions

Harmony is important

Perceiving

Flexible and spontaneous

Adapt to what is going on

Open to possibilities

Judging

Like planning and order

Like to make decisions

Sense of control

These preferences can sit alongside your DISC results (see page 53), so you can start to recognize your behaviour and how you interact.

Personality and growth mindset

It has been suggested that personality traits tend to be fixed, but as a fan of growth mindset I believe that you can change elements of your personality if you have the drive and desire to do so. Carol Dweck, psychologist, educator and author of *Mindset* spoke about her research into this at a conference I attended in 2019, where students were able to reduce their levels of aggression (a personality trait) by adopting a growth mindset approach: they were told to believe that they were able to change and develop less aggressive thinking and behaviour and the evidence showed they were! This thinking forms the basis of most rehabilitation programmes worldwide and I strongly believe that if you want to change, you can.

The basis of behavioural change through neuroplasticity is as follows:

1) Consider what you want to change.
2) Identify why it is important to you and access your motivation. A great exercise is to imagine that you have changed this element of your personality: What is different? How are you different? What are you feeling? What are you thinking? When you go to this future state, you are priming your brain for change as you start to build connections between your neurons, creating a new neural pathway.
3) Think about what you can do to support the new behaviour – for example, if you want to be calmer what are the small behaviours that you can start practising each day? You might start practicing mindfulness with a 10-minute session every day, or you might look at your

diary and give yourself time between tasks, or you might start practicing gratitude with a journal each evening, or you might reduce the amount you look at your phone and social media. Every time we practise, we are strengthening the neural pathway which is re-wiring our brain.

4) Each day, do something which connects to the new behaviour you want to create. If you consider the example above: if you spend 10 minutes a day practicing mindfulness or start a gratitude journal, after a month you will see a difference in your thinking. As James Clear, habit expert and author, would say this is building a compound effect and it is working in our brains to make the new neural pathway our preferred pathway.

5) Reflect on how you feel each week and add in a new behaviour to support the new way of being – for example, if you decided to feel calmer, your first week may be focused on the gratitude practice and then you might add reducing time on your phone by putting it in another room.

Dopamine hit

This re-wiring process can be supercharged when you add in a positive emotional response following the new behaviour. Even a small response releases dopamine, which is connected to pleasure. When your brain makes a connection between a behaviour and pleasure, it starts to anticipate the dopamine hit and therefore the behaviour is encouraged. You can experience this positive emotion by giving yourself a positive reward. This will be more effective if you do something which is congruent and aligns with the behaviour you are looking to create – for example, you want to be calmer and therefore meditate each day for 10 minutes. After your meditation, you reward yourself with a herbal tea, which also enables you to feel calm (coffee may have the opposite effect!).

REFLECTION

If you are unsure about what you want to change, try journalling using these prompts:

- How do you feel about your personality preferences?
- What did you find out about yourself today?
- How will this impact how you interact with others?
- What elements of your personality do you hide or decrease?
- How would it be different if you embraced these?
- What would you like to change about your personality?

When I first started my business as a coach, I felt that I had to dial down my natural drive and ambition (my D in DISC), as these were not desirable traits to share. Instead of being confident in who I am and my preferences, I didn't talk about my determination to succeed due to a fear of being judged. The irony is that I attracted a lot of my clients at the time because of my drive and goal-oriented focus – they wanted to "borrow" these traits and step into my energy with them.

What others think

There will always be people who think you are too much or not enough. Perhaps they are triggered by you as you remind them of elements of their personality that they may not like or of people they haven't liked in the past. You can either respond by putting on a mask and exaggerating certain traits, or you can accept who you are and focus on what you can control, learning to let go of what others think of you. When you do this, you will start to step into who you are.

Contrary to popular belief, there is no one right way to be. Part of the process of self-coaching and self-development is about accepting everything about yourself so that you're confident in your behaviour. When you play to your preferences and stand boldly in the shadow as well as the light, you become more magnetic to others.

Overcoming people pleasing.

We often "wear a mask" to please others due to a fear of rejection or being left out, and to avoid conflict. On an subconscious level, you make decisions about whether you are "in group" or "out of group" all the time, as your brain is flagging that some people are "safe" and like you while some are "unsafe" and not like you. Your brain is wired to move away from threat or danger and toward pleasure – it's normal to want to "fit in" to the group.

Over the years I have worked with many clients who are people pleasers. They care deeply about what others think and adjust their behaviour to suit those around them, desperate to ensure that they don't upset people. When you play this role, you put others' needs before your own. Eventually this leads to resentment and you find that your "pleasing" behaviours aren't really "pleasing" anyone. As a reformed people pleaser, I know that breaking this habit can be difficult and feel uncomfortable. But I can reassure you that instead of always second-guessing what others want or need from you, if you are authentically and consistently yourself, then your relationships and confidence will improve.

I have helped many clients, who are stuck in people pleasing, identify a new way of being. This has enabled them to make decisions based on what is best for them and to have more meaningful relationships, as well as reduce the responsibility they felt for others, which helped them to feel happier and calmer. You can do this too.

Being authentic

Authenticity is about connecting to who you are and your self-awareness. Often you go through life on autopilot, going through the motions without consideration or reflection.

When I was a deputy head, I got up every day, went to work, did my job, came home and went to bed, until the weekend when I drank wine (often excessively). On the surface it looked like I was connected but, in reality, I was going through the motions as though I was on autopilot. The wine was a reward for "getting through the week". As soon as Monday came around, I was counting down the days till the weekend again.

For most of the time at work, I was wearing a mask and behaving how I believed I "should". The weekend wine gave me a release to exhale and be myself or at least take off the mask. What I wasn't doing was giving myself time to process or explore my feelings on a deeper level, which is why I felt a sense of disconnection.

Increasing your self-awareness

How do you start to get to know yourself better? Imagine you are dating yourself, what traits would you see straight away? Then as the weeks, months and years go by, what would come out? Often at the beginning of relationships people work hard to ensure they are presenting the best version of themselves and it can be exhausting. Over time, the mask slips as this "ideal self" can't be sustained forever – soon the honeymoon period becomes a distant memory. I am sure you have witnessed this not only in romantic relationships, but also in personal ones, where the person you initially met seems very different from the one you know now.

REFLECTION

Journal your responses to the prompts below and you will start to see what you have been hiding from others and how that can stop you showing up as authentically you.

- When I first meet someone, I want them to think ...
- I don't want them to think ...
- I wouldn't want most people knowing ...
- When I meet new people, I do my best to hide ...
- Often people are surprised when they learn ...
- I wish I didn't ...

You can't wear a mask forever. A lot of people in their mid-30s upwards come to coaching to connect with who they are. About 80 per cent of my clients and a similar percentage of the people who come to me to train as a coach are in this age group.

Around 70 per cent of people say that they want to increase their self-awareness, and 40 per cent increase their self-acceptance through coaching. This evidence is backed up by conversations that I have with clients and through our training programmes. My clients tend to have lightbulb moments when they realize that they have been hiding who they are as a way to help them to fit in and be accepted. They often share that because they have been wearing a mask for so long, they don't truly know who they are anymore. If this resonates with you, be reassured that you will have a much clearer idea of who you are by the end of the book!

REFLECTION

Over the next week when you have a problem to solve, take some time out and do something different. Then reflect on:
- When you got your best ideas
- What you need to be more creative in your thinking

Making changes

When you have become aware of something, hopefully through reflecting and journalling, it is worth then asking yourself "So, what?". It is great to have the learning, but what are you going to start doing differently as a result?

For example, to build in time to think more effectively:

- If you know that you get great ideas when you are walking, how can you schedule time in your diary each week to walk in nature?
- If you know that you get great ideas when you visit art galleries, when can you schedule time to do this?

This is about leaning forward into tangible actions and making a plan to ensure that you execute them. Scheduling time is a good first point. In coaching, this is the final part of any session and focuses on what the client will do in-between sessions to embed their learning. It is the actions that the client chooses to do which build the neural pathways and help ensure behaviours are effectively embedded.

Self-acceptance

A big part of reconnecting to yourself and increasing your self-awareness is about self-acceptance; you are dropping the negative self-talk and instead accepting who you are right now. This is where a growth mindset comes in handy. You will find things which you aren't as good at, but when you approach these from a viewpoint that you haven't yet mastered them, and see yourself as the student rather than criticizing yourself for a lack of ability, it makes a huge difference to how you show up. While it may well be that you aren't as good at some things, you can choose how you speak to yourself about this.

When I accepted what I wasn't good at, everything changed. I realized that I wasn't very good at day-to-day management because my strength is bigger picture thinking rather than detail. I looked at how I could run and lead a team more efficiently and who around me was making some key decisions about how to run my business, rather than beating myself up about why I couldn't do it effectively. This meant that I hired for the gaps in my skillset, delegating what I wasn't doing well and working with my own coach to develop some of my skills.

The key here is speaking to yourself with compassion, rather than allowing your inner critic to rule the roost (see page 28). Even when you make a mistake, you can still be kind to yourself.

If someone in a restaurant gets your order wrong, you wouldn't shout at them and tell them they were useless (at least I hope you wouldn't), so what makes you talk to yourself in that way?

Realize that you are already enough, right now in this moment. Wanting more for yourself, or committing to the journey of personal growth, doesn't take away from that. Wherever you are – maybe you are lying in bed with your PJs on or are on a train on the way to work reading this – just sit with that thought. Sounds simple doesn't it? Test it out in your head: if I am already enough, then what does that mean? How can I grow from where I am, secure in the knowledge that my roots are there to hold me up and support my growth?

When I work with clients, I support them to change the measure of themselves from "perfect" to "good enough". Aiming for perfection has made many of them stop taking any action at all. Consider your friends and those who you love: how many of them are perfect? Perfection is a myth which keeps all of us small.

Like anything, you can't wave a magic wand and be all Zen about who you are. This process takes time and energy and is a step toward where you want to be and lasting change. "The work" is continuous small steps toward your end goal.

This feeling of self-acceptance is a great foundation to build from and help you realize that you don't need to spend your time focusing on how you can conform. Of course, we have social and societal norms which govern how we behave (such as saying please and thank you, queueing etc). What I'm talking about is being comfortable with being you, rather than thinking you must be more or less of anything.

REFLECTION

Journal using these prompts. If I felt good enough right now:

- What would I be thinking?
- What would I be feeling?
- How would I feel in my body?
- What would I be doing more of?
- What would I be doing less of?
- Where do I feel that I am enough?
- What would be different in my life?

Your needs

It's time to revisit the iceberg (see page 2) and look at what is underneath. You have looked at your personality preferences and now it is time to explore some other dimensions that can impact how you show up and behave. Your needs refer to your basic survival strategies. At some level, all of us function to feel safe and secure – have shelter and warmth. If you're in a situation where any of these needs are threatened, whether through job, financial or relationship insecurity, it will affect how you show up. This is because our nervous system is activated and you will be sent into fight, flight or freeze mode.

Maslow's Hierarchy of Needs

This pyramid model, developed by the psychologist Abraham Maslow, is a way of helping you to classify your needs into different categories. They are a continuum and you are going up level by level through the pyramid. Number one is the bottom of the pyramid and five at the top.

1) **Physiological needs:** These include food, water, warmth and rest. If these basic needs are not being met, then you are not going to be looking at your purpose and mission in life – your primary driver is to feel safe. For you, this may include having the money to pay your rent or mortgage, or being able to afford to eat well.

2) **Safety needs:** When we don't feel safe in our home life, relationships or work life, we can often go into fight, flight or freeze mode.

3) **Love and belonging needs:** This is the first of our psychological needs. We need to have relationships with others to feel connected and valued.

4) **Esteem needs**: The next psychological need is for prestige and a feeling of accomplishment.

5) **Self-actualization:** This is a need to feel that we are realizing and using all our talents, and living a life which has meaning and purpose.

Assessing your needs

Go back to the Wheel of Life exercise (see page 8) and think about the areas that you identified. Now consider for each area which of your needs are currently being met e.g., if you are feeling financially secure, it may mean that your physiological and safety needs are being met. However, if you are struggling with your relationship and you aren't feeling safe and secure, you may be struggling with safety needs. If your basic needs are met, the hope is that you are meeting some of the other needs all the way up to self-actualization.

Remember this is how you feel about your needs and how they are being met, rather than someone else's observations.

Add whatever you discover onto the Wheel of Life document so that you start building a picture of what you want to change in each of the categories.

When I have worked with clients who are in a "threat" state, where they feel that they are not able to pay their mortgage, then there is a huge impact on their ability to achieve other goals. This is because the anticipated threat of danger, such as feeling you can't feed yourself or that you may not be able to pay your rent, puts you into a threat response which means that the energy is taken away from your executive function (thinking, problem-solving, memory) to deal with the stressor. The sympathetic nervous system is activated so we go into fight, flight, freeze or fawn. If you are in this state, I would advise you to get some support and make a plan as it can be incredibly difficult cognitively to think clearly. Do seek support (see page 264).

Equally, if you are in any situation where you don't feel psychologically secure, it can impact your wellbeing and your ability to really step into your purpose. If this is a relationship at home, consider how you can get support. If it is at work, then it is worth talking to your manager and HR department. Remember that you have the right to feel safe and secure; our psychological safety and wellbeing are critical to us feeling better.

Beyond basic needs
Tony Robbins, a motivational speaker, and Cloe Madanes, a teacher of Family Therapy, came up with their own version

of needs. This categorization exercise can build on the work you have done with Maslow. I like this exercise because it goes beyond basic needs and helps you identify what is most important to you. This can link to your personality and behavioural preferences – for example, those who score highly on I in DISC (see page 50) may have more of a need for uncertainty, whereas those who score highly on S may have more of a need for certainty.

I see this as building a picture of who you are across different dimensions, with your personality and behavioural preferences at the heart of who you are right now. Then the other dimensions add into this colourful exploration of the essence of you. Needs tend to be more flexible than behavioural preferences, as the importance of these will change over time and based on your circumstances, as will which needs are being met and where you need to focus your time. There is more of a fluidity with them as you can feel that these are things which you have control over changing, in some cases in the immediate future.

What I like about this system is that it takes into account that we all have a differing blend of needs at any given time – for example, if you have just started a new job, you may want certainty that you are doing the right thing and contributing to the business. If you are in a new relationship, you may be enjoying the uncertainty of what will come next and the spontaneity of the first parts of romance. In time, you may want more certainty that the relationship will last. Examining the six different dimensions opposite can be useful when looking at what you need in a situation, as it helps you to start to think about what you already have and what may be lacking. It can also help you to make sense of your behaviour.

Six Human Needs

This is an exercise created by Tony Robbins and Cloe Madanes. Read through each of these areas and consider how you feel about each one and what you may need to focus on e.g., you may reflect on the fact that you need more certainty in your life than you currently have, and consider how you will get this.

1. **Certainty:** The degree to which you believe that you know what is going to happen next. The desire for predictability.
2. **Uncertainty:** The degree to which you desire variety and excitement in your life.
3. **Significance:** The degree to which you feel like you belong and matter to others.
4. **Connection**: The degree to which you feel you have close relationships with both yourself and others.
5. **Growth:** The degree to which you feel like you are developing and improving personally and professionally.
6. **Contribution:** The degree to which you feel like you are adding to others' lives and impacting others positively.

It is common to be labelled "needy" and in this exercise you can see the context: maybe you want to have more contact with friends or a loved one as you are not feeling like your desire for connection is being met. Or you want to know what is happening at work as you are craving more certainty in your life. The interesting part is that when you feel out of kilter in one area of your life, which was perhaps demonstrated in your Wheel of Life (see page 8), you may realize it is because a need that is important to you is not being met. Looking back at your Wheel of Life, does that ring true for you?

REFLECTION

Journal using these prompts:
- What needs do I feel are being met?
- What needs do I feel I need to focus on?
- How will I focus on these?

Values and motivation: What drives you?

When your needs are met, you can move toward looking at your values, which are what drive or dictate your behaviour. They are like an inner compass and may be partly reflected in your personality preference. When things are important to you, they motivate you intrinsically. If you are doing work or living your life in congruence with your internal drivers, you are much more likely to be successful and feel true to yourself.

How do you do this? You need to make sure you understand what your values are: what are the things that are truly important to you? When you complete the values exercise opposite make sure that you are honest. Remember, there is no judgement around values! On social media, people love to shout about how they are authentic or have integrity – words are great but values go deeper. They are your way of being and, when your needs are met, your values drive your behaviour.

I've found that clients often tick the values which they feel they *should* be rather than what they are. As I was seeing clients coming up with the same sorts of lists, or struggling with the exercise, I looked at alternative ways to help identify values and came across the work of John Demartini, author and consultant. This informs my approach and I believe it is more insightful.

Here you look at a variety of options, such as where you spend your time and your money, so you can start to see what's important to you. It is easy to make inferences about someone who works 80 hours a week and only sees their family at weekends. However, if you are able to explore this, you may find that they work these long hours to provide safety and security for their family because that is what's important to them. Someone else might be in the role of a traditional home-maker, as they see this as a way of getting safety and security.

Our values may well come from our early experiences of what we saw was important or "valued" around us, and therefore two people with very different personality preferences may hold a similar set of values. Shared values are often seen as more of a determining factor in long-term relationships, which is why institutions like the Catholic Church include values exercises as part of their marriage preparation classes. What's important to you appears to be a bigger determinant of your relationships and friendships than how you express yourself.

Values-based questions

In this exercise, you are asked a variety of questions related to your behaviour to help you determine your values and what is important to you:

- Where do you spend your time?
- What do you spend your money on?

- Where do you wish you could spend more time?
- Where do you most enjoy spending your time?
- If you had more money, what would you spend it on?
- What do you feel drives these behaviours and spending habits?
- From this exercise, what do you think is most important to you?

When you have answered these questions, you should have a good idea of what drives you. How these values are expressed is often down to your behavioural and personality preferences e.g., if you value freedom as someone who is high on extroversion, it may well mean being spontaneous and spending time with groups of people; if you're high on introversion, it might be freedom to spend time on your own reading or walking. When you look at that list of values, ask yourself, "How much am I living a life which is congruent with these values right now?" If you're not in alignment with your values, or you are in conflict, it's going to be a hard slog to get anything done. It may be that doing this exercise in itself was an eye opener as your behaviours can be out of sync with the life you want to create. The more that you're able to tune into your values and really understand how you can personify them, the more you can move forward with flow and ease.

Strengths

The final stage in getting to know yourself is identifying your strengths. Your behavioural preferences from DISC (see page 50) may inform this thinking, for example, if you were high on C preferences, you'll be stronger at analytical thinking; if you are high on I preferences, big picture thinking and vision are a strength. Strengths-based coaching starts with identifying what you really love doing and are better at than others. Positive psychologists, such as Martin Seligman, encourage people to look at building strengths and I love this approach. Most education systems cultivate the idea that you need to be good at everything. There is an expectation that you can do Maths, English and French, alongside Drama, Music and Art, with a side dose of sports, alongside being sociable, outgoing, confident and a great friend. The truth is you'll have areas where you're stronger than others and when you play to those strengths, and build on them, you will be more effective than if you were to spend endless hours trying to improve things you aren't so good at. Of course, growth mindset states you can always improve and get better; you can improve anything, however, it's worth focusing on what you enjoy and are good at as the gains will be more significant and it will be more fun!

When I was a deputy headteacher, like many schools in the UK, the driving force at mine was to get as many students their GCSE grades, including English and Maths, as possible. When students were not at the level that they needed to be, they were given more work. I remember one student saying to me, "Miss, I don't like Thursdays so I won't come in." When I asked why, she said "I have five out of six lessons which are Maths and I hate Maths". By giving her more of what she didn't like, and wasn't good at, we had effectively driven her out of school. A lesson there for sure!

REFLECTION

To help identify your strengths, consider the following reflection questions:

- What are the activities that you can do where time becomes elastic?
- What would you do for work, if you could only do one thing for the rest of your life?

When you are looking at your strengths, consider how you can apply them to how you want to live your life. Your strengths are the transferable skills that recruiters love and they can be utilized in many different ways. You naturally want to play to your strengths, so your behavioural preferences will be underpinned by them – for example, if you are detail focused and precise, your preference is to do this work and you would be higher in C in DISC (see page 50). If you are driven by achieving goals, you would be higher in D preference. Strengths also interact with values as we tend to work on the things that we think are important and express these through our strengths.

I see the needs/values/strengths idea working as a pyramid. At the bottom are our needs; when they are not met or are in conflict, they can drive our behaviour. This will often be in a fight, flight or freeze situation, where we are unable to clearly define what is important to us or have the cognitive space to work on our strengths. When you know what your values are, and are aligned with these both at home and work, you can look at playing to your strengths. The system can collapse when we are put in environments where we feel unsafe or where our values are threatened, which can then activate our stress and nervous system response.

When you look at the bigger context and the work of Maslow and Madanes and Robbins, you realize that the "meaning" or self-actualization elements are met when you are playing to your strengths and working in congruence with your values. This is the space you aspire to be in, in both your professional and personal life.

I have been in so many situations where this hasn't been the case and a number of elements may be at play:

- Personality clashes
- Being in environments where our needs aren't met
- Values clashes
- Not feeling like we are playing to our strengths

All these elements impact how you feel and what you're thinking, as well as your behaviour. When you know yourself better, you can start to see what is happening and it can be liberating.

Another great way to assess your strengths is to reflect back on when you've been the happiest and most successful. When you're playing to your strengths, you are often in that "flow" state and you're likely to be achieving more, so the reflection questions on the opposite page can help you to get clarity on what you're good at! You can find your strengths hard to determine as they are things which can come easily, but when you find them it can be a lightbulb moment. My advice is to not discredit things you feel are easy; they are often easy to you as they are strengths.

I have been a teacher or a coach since I was 23, starting off as a scuba-diving instructor. I then became a recruiter, where I coached candidates in interview skills, before training as a teacher. I had other jobs, but it was always teaching/ training/coaching that I came back to, as these skills come easily to me. When I am in this role, I feel energized and engaged. I have taught in various ways: in schools, as a tutor, as a trainer, to business owners, and I started up my business using my skills. Transferable skills are a buzzword for a reason; you can take skills from different areas of your life and use them elsewhere.

Understanding your strengths

This is an exercise I use with clients to help them begin to get clarity on their strengths.

Ask five people who know you really well to feedback on:
- What they think you are really good at
- Three words they would use to describe you

Now reflect on the answers they gave you:
- What do you feel when you see these words?
- What do you think is missing?
- What would you take out?

What do you feel are your core strengths after doing this exercise?

Flow state

When you're playing to your strengths, you often experience flow state, which is when you're doing something that comes naturally and easily to you. Start to notice when you are in flow. When you are in this state, external validation isn't needed, but getting that validation is always an indicator of when you're shining your light brighter in some area of your life and is something to explore further.

Gay Hendricks, author of *The Big Leap*, talks about the different zones that we can inhabit. The four zones are: incompetence, competence, excellence and genius. In the Chapter 1 exercise where you drew out the activities that you liked, didn't mind and disliked (see page 19), I bet that the dislikes are in your zone of incompetence, the don't minds are in your zone of competence and the zone of excellence, and the likes are in your zone of genius. The big defining feature of the zone of genius is you are good at these things and you love doing them.

Martin Seligman, positive psychologist, suggests that when you play to your strengths you don't need the same level of external accountability – for example, you probably get tasks completed at work to meet deadlines. You may do things at home to look after others. When you're truly playing to your strengths, you do things because you love them and become engrossed in them.

This isn't only about your working life. When we play to our strengths in all areas of our lives, we feel happier – for example, you may be very organized and enjoy planning holidays, whereas your partner or friends may dislike this. The more we know about what we enjoy and are good at, the more we can use our strengths in all areas. This is about building on that reflective practice and getting curious about the patterns that you notice in your behaviour and how you feel.

REFLECTION

If you are still stuck, then ask yourself these reflection questions:

- What do you keep coming back to?
- What do people come to you for?
- When do you feel most content?

These questions should help you build on this work.

Connecting to all elements of you

This chapter has been designed to help you to go deeper beneath the iceberg, through the lens of personality and behavioural preferences and then through the lens of your needs, values and strengths. You will have increased your self-awareness and started to recognize patterns of behaviour and where they stem from. Hopefully, you will have also begun to be more self-accepting and realized that you can show up as authentically you.

This work will help you answer the question "Where are you now?" in more detail. In Step Two, you will be looking at where you want to be and then, in Step Three, finding a path to get there. I want to remind you that you're not what has happened to you in the past, and you don't have to be who you have been before. You might have made decisions that didn't work out or failed to stand up for yourself and felt resentful of this. It's time to make peace with the past; there is nothing you can do about it now.

The exercises you have done in Step One, with the Wheel of Life at the heart, are your starting point and this will then form your next iteration and evolution. You can't change what you can't measure – now you will have a good measure of what you can change!

Remember, you get to choose how you want to be in the future and make the changes from those foundations you now know so much more about.

KEY POINTS TO REMEMBER

- Self-awareness is the key to change.
- We all have different personality and behavioural preferences – understanding yours can help you to build your self-awareness and improve relationships.
- We are fundamentally driven by our needs being met; if they are unmet, it is hard to focus on values and strengths.
- Our values are our GPS – they guide our behaviour, and affect how we show up and what is important to us.
- Strengths define what we are good at; when we play to these, we are often happier and more fulfilled.

STEP TWO

Get Clear on Where You Want to Be

In this section you will explore what you want your life to look like. It's time to answer the question "Where do I want to be?" You will be learning about the power of positive visualization to strengthen those neural pathways and combining this approach with more practical goal-setting techniques, so that you're transforming thinking into action.

By looking at "the big dream", you work with the reward centre in your amygdala, which releases dopamine, as it associates your positive future state with pleasure – the more frequently you visualize, the more you are reinforcing what's important to you. Equally, stepping into future-focused thinking enhances your executive function: problem-solving, decision-making, deep thinking and memory – the processes which lie in the brain's prefrontal cortex and hippocampus. This is all about working with your brain to create a clear picture of what's next so you have a map to follow.

As a coach, I believe that you have all the resources that you need inside of you. This means that you're capable of making decisions and doing difficult things. Seeing yourself as capable is empowering – you are in the driving seat, you decide what happens. Keep this in mind as you encounter challenges.

The big questions you will address in Step Two are:

- **What do you want in your life?** You will be looking at using vision boards and visualization techniques, as well as the "Be, Do, Have" planning tool to help you get clarity on what you want.
- **How can you break down your big vision into actionable goals?** You will be making your big thinking

tangible by setting SMART goals, which you can use to assess your progress.

- **How do you need to be?** By looking at success habits, you will be building a solid foundation which will help you to achieve your goals.

This is your chance to step into your dreams and start to get crystal clear on what you want your future to hold. It can make you feel supercharged as you work with the positive emotional attractors (PEAs) in your brain, which enhance your thinking. If you need a lift at any point when you are taking action or integrating, revisit this part of the book and spend time connecting to who you want to be. This might be when you are feeling less motivated or you are not moving forward as quickly as you want to. Connecting to your big vision helps to increase motivation and positivity, which enhances wellbeing as well as giving you that dopamine boost.

You will be building on the activities in Part 1, as you move from the present toward the future. I will remind you to refer back to them, so you can start to see the connections.

Being limitless

It's time to think big, get out of your past ways of thinking about what is or isn't possible and step into who you truly want to be. Imagine that you didn't feel the personal or societal limitations that you do now and that you could do whatever you wanted to. In this section, I am encouraging you to think like Disney and we will go through the "Disney-thinking" models, working from imagination through to reality.

It might feel like a leap going from your day-to-day reality to big thinking. Big visions can sometimes feel overwhelming and here is the thing: it's our brain keeping us safe and realistic. When you think about the reasons why it won't work, you activate the nervous system and put yourself into threat mode. You may notice yourself thinking, "This is not going to happen for me because of ...". When you get trapped in this thinking, it can prevent you from moving toward change. That is why I encourage you to be aware of that inner critic and focus on possibility before getting practical and looking at action.

I tell my clients I want them to go to the edge to feel like they're in a HIIT class and about to be sick, but to stop just before they get there. Why? Well, change doesn't happen for our bodies or our minds when we play it safe. Safe means safe results; it doesn't mean transformation. Take yourself to that feeling where you are on the edge and ask yourself, "What would doing this thing bring me?".

Remember that your emotions are linked to what's happened before and they're often attached to situations to keep you safe. Imagine you didn't have those restrictions blocking your way. How does that feel? How does that big vision connect into your purpose and your body? Where are you feeling the fizz of the vision and where are you feeling resistance? The more that you can learn to tune into the intuitive feelings that you have in your body, the more that you can move forward.

When you can connect deeply with how you want to be, imagine you are that version of you speaking to you right now. What advice would you give? How would you show up differently if you knew that this version of you was there waiting? How would you be different? Connect with what you will do first and start doing it.

When I decided to commit to starting my business, I was about to go on maternity leave with my second daughter. At the time, I had no experience of the online world and was barely on social media. I imagined working for myself and being able to be around for my children more, as well as doing a job I loved (and ditching the politics which I didn't love). It didn't seem possible, but a part of me thought "what the hell" and I went for it. Five months into maternity leave, I resigned from my job and committed to the business – this would never have happened if I hadn't started imagining that it was possible.

Visions and actions

When I started my business, daily visualization helped me to reprogram my brain to see the possibility; daily action meant that possibility became my reality. It really is that simple. This works because the brain is unable to distinguish between thoughts and reality so, if you start to imagine that you are at a specific place, you are creating a new neural pathway in the brain. The more that you focus on your new reality, the more you strengthen the neural pathway and increase the likelihood of this happening.

After securing your big vision and where you want to go, I advocate starting small in terms of your actions and building consistently. This is the opposite of the "get rich quick" approach and is all about achieving sustainable change. Making big changes is hard and can take you so far out of your comfort zone that your nervous system is activated and you are back in fight, flight, freeze or fawn (see page 3). Instead, I want you to take gradual steps and embed the change in your brain (and finally, the basal ganglia) so it sticks.

This small-step approach reminds me of the Desmond Tutu quote: "There is only one way to eat an elephant: a bite at a time". You are chopping up your big vision into bite-size chunks, keeping the end goal in mind as you build through consistency. If you think that your big vision is your guiding star, it will help motivate you and keep you on track.

Flexibility

Remember that the best-laid plans don't always work out, so be open to fluidity and re-evaluation. When I was writing this, I checked in with my Facebook memories: one of them was written in October 2019 when I was promoting an event to plan "Your best ever 2020". I had planned three retreats and a big event at a stately home. It turned out the world had other ideas. Great businesses set out their short-, medium- and long-term plans and strategy, then review and re-evaluate them regularly to allow the option of changing course and responding to what is going on externally (such as a pandemic!). Being able to adapt and be flexible in your approach is one of the ways you will be successful – it is one of the things which has kept me on track throughout my life as I realize that roadblocks and obstacles are always there to teach us something, however hard it is at the time.

Belief

One of the key things to work on in this section is your belief. As Henry Ford famously said, "Whether you believe you can, or think you can't, you're right". If you don't believe something is possible for you, then you aren't going to take action. This doesn't mean you need to be always thinking you are unstoppable; doubts will come in at times. Remind yourself that this is your brain's way of keeping you safe. Your belief is like a muscle; the more you work it, the stronger it gets. All you need at this point is to believe in the possibility that this could happen for you.

For years I did this simple exercise each morning. When I woke up, I asked myself where I was on a scale of 1–10 in terms of my self-belief and then I thought about the one thing I could do to get closer to a 10. At the start, I was pretty low down at a one or two, but over time I saw a huge difference in how I felt about myself – all from this very simple exercise. The things I were doing were simple: asking for help, sharing my story, speaking to my husband, doing a quick workout, looking at feedback and journalling. They were the first bricks in the wall. I encourage you to do the same – do one thing first thing in the morning and it will set you up for the day. Again, this is about focusing on building change in your brain by re-wiring the neural pathways.

You can revisit and revise as you go. I tend to step into a new way of being and doing (and having), then I go back and think bigger – for example, I set an intention of moving to a new area of London about five years before we did. As we explored the areas, we had our minds set on somewhere but lockdown happened and we realised how much outside space mattered, so we looked at being closer to Epping Forest, in a slightly different area than we had initially been looking at. I revised my vision to change as we had felt a shift in our needs and, a couple of years later, we moved into our dream house opposite the forest. Your vision may change as life happens and that is okay; you don't need to stay fixed on things that no longer work for you.

Desire and purpose

When you dig into your desires for the future, you are likely to realize that the superyachts and flashy cars are not your drivers for success. Although we are all motivated by financial success to some degree, the driving force is often a desire to meet your needs, as described by Maslow (see page 67). Although money provides stability and security, after a certain point you realize that it isn't giving you more happiness. This is often when my clients come to me, wanting to connect more with their purpose.

This is backed up by research by psychologist Daniel Kahneman.[7] In 2010, he found that emotional wellbeing rose with income until people reached an annual salary of $75,000 (at current levels, this would be $90,000 or around £75,000). However, when people earned over this level, there was no increase in emotional wellbeing. Although higher income did correlate with higher levels of life satisfaction, it didn't with happiness. This doesn't mean you should put down the book if you aren't at the income level for peak wellbeing because you can always improve how you feel. I'm sharing this point because I see it in my client work; many people come to me for coaching because they don't feel happy after earning the bigger money and realize they have been chasing the wrong things. Maybe this resonates with you.

Remember, plans are there as a starting point. It's hard to find a destination unless we put it on the satnav (anyone remember maps?) and it's the same with your life. Of course, we can be open to possibilities, road closures and roadblocks but having some kind of direction is better than none.

STEP TWO AIMS

- This is your chance to dream big and start to connect with where you want to be.
- You may find it difficult to imagine big changes – it is OK to start small.
- You can revisit and revise over time – remember you are getting to know yourself and what feels good.
- Plans are there as a starting point; they don't have to be written in stone.
- If a complete life overhaul is overwhelming, start with one area first.
- Revisiting the exercises in Step One can be useful to help you to focus.

4

Visualization, Vision, Future Self

This is your opportunity to get really creative with your future and start to imagine how you want things to be. I encourage you to take your time with this process as it might not be as simple as sitting down with a pen and paper and everything flowing out with ease; although if this happens, brilliant! If it doesn't, this is your invitation to take it slower and to spend time engaging with your creativity. This part of the process is "value tagging", which helps tell your brain and subconscious what to focus on. By commanding your brain in this way, you're more likely to open up to opportunities. This works along the same principle as when you are thinking of buying a particular car and then you see that make of car all the time; they have always been there, but your brain now knows they are important to you, so you recognize them.

In this chapter you will explore how to:

- Identify your desires
- Gain clarity on your vision
- Identify elements of wellbeing
- Create your vision board

- Benefit from visualization
- Commit to a daily visualization practice

Vision, purpose and mission

Vision is the ability to think or plan for a future with imagination and wisdom. It's a word you hear a lot, whether in the context of a managing director talking about where they see the company going, or in looking at your own life and your guiding principles.

By painting a clear picture of where you are heading, you are more likely to get there. As renowned author and motivational speaker Steven Covey says "Begin with the end in mind" – this will enable you to plan your journey and route to success. Equally, when you know where you are headed it can motivate you as you move toward the desired outcome. Our brains love direction!

A defined sense of vision can link to your mission and help ground you in what you want to do to move forward. Often, it's this freedom to step out of your day-to-day goals and into purpose and dreaming that helps you get out of your head and connect with your desires. The big picture connects with your deeper purpose and what's important, building on your values work (see page 72).

Going back to Maslow's Hierarchy of Needs (see page 67), achieving purpose is when you reach self-actualization (the top of the pyramid). You can't live according to your purpose if you have unmet needs. I ask clients to consider if:

- Their needs are met
- They are living in congruence to their values
- They are playing to their strengths

- They are feeling happy and engaged in what they
  are doing

Purpose is often seen as being related to career. I believe it is when you feel that what you are doing has meaning and is therefore valuable.

Increasing your sense of wellbeing

There is evidence that when you connect to your sense of purpose, it increases your overall feelings of wellbeing, as described by psychologist Dr Martin Seligman in his PERMA model for wellbeing. In this model, Seligman says that wellbeing can be measured by looking at five separate elements:

P – Positive Emotion: The frequency of feeling positive emotions.

E – Engagement: How present and engaged you are in activities and what you are doing.

R – Relationships: The extent to which you feel supported and connected with others.

M – Meaning or Purpose: How much you feel what you do is connected to something bigger.

A – Accomplishments: The extent to which you recognize and celebrate what you achieve.

Each of these measures add up to a wellbeing score and each area can be developed. This model is a fantastic way of auditing where you are and committing to some actions, building on the work you did on your needs and values in Step One.

P – Positive Emotion

You can increase the frequency of positive emotions by looking at the past, present and future.

Past: Practising Forgiveness and Gratitude

You can increase positive emotion by practising forgiveness and gratitude.

Forgiveness: It sounds easy to say that if you forgive you feel better, but how do you do it? One way is to write a letter to yourself or others forgiving them for their part in what has happened. When you have written the letter, sit with the emotions that you feel. By this I mean, take time to experience them, whatever they are; this may mean that you cry or feel angry or resentful. These emotions are a way of processing what has happened. Then, when you feel ready, go back and re-write the letter until you are at a point where you can feel neutral about the people and the situation. This process could take weeks; each time you revisit it, consider the growth that you have experienced and celebrate this.

Writing about past negative experiences has positive outcomes for how you feel. In her 2019 research on the effects of expressive writing, Brynne DiMenichi, neuroscientist and clinical researcher, found the experience of writing about something negative decreases feelings of depression and anxiety and has a positive impact on physical health and cognitive performance.[8] By writing about a negative experience, situation or feeling, you're able to process this in the brain which then helps you to move on.

Using the same principles as the forgiveness letter, on retreats, I get my clients to write down the things they want to let go of in the form of a letter to someone (or themselves) offering forgiveness. We then burn these letters in a ceremony to help let go of the feelings of resentment, anger and negativity. For example, imagine you have had a bad break up and are still feeling anger, hurt and resentment toward your ex-partner. These emotions are not serving you and may be stopping you from moving on. By working through your emotions in a letter, you can make sense of them and start to process them, helping you to forgive. When we can forgive ourselves and others, it helps us to let go of unhelpful emotions and attachments to people or situations.

Practising the art of forgiveness helps you to process what has happened more effectively, so you can let go of some of the unhelpful negative emotions you may have been unconsciously holding onto. This is congruent with the work I do as a spiral energy practitioner. I work with clients to help clear their attachment to negative emotions.

Gratitude: There is evidence that gratitude journalling and practising gratitude can increase positive affect (the extent to which we experience positive emotions) as it produces the neurotransmitters serotonin and dopamine. Serotonin is linked to positive mood and happiness, and is what makes people feel euphoric when taking ecstasy tablets. You won't be having those levels of euphoria, but practising gratitude is a step toward you feeling a natural "high", which is really the basis for this book – feeling better by understanding your body and your brain more effectively and working with them. By building in a daily gratitude practice, you are helping to re-wire your brain and build new neural pathways linked to positive affect making you feel better.

There is evidence that gratitude journalling increases positive emotions and decreases feelings of depression,[9] therefore supporting Seligman's model (see page 95). I use gratitude when I want to get out of a funk e.g., when I wake up and feel a bit "meh", I practice gratitude in my head as a reset and I'm able to change how I feel. When I have had a bad day at work or have heard that someone has said something negative about me, I again revisit gratitude. I go on gratitude walks; I put on my trainers, walk into the forest and stomp to get rid of my anger/frustration/annoyance and then talk to myself about what I am grateful for. I find that moving my body helps me to get out of my head and regulates my sympathetic nervous system, so I can think more effectively and the gratitude cheers me up. You can't be stressed and grateful at the same time, so I highly recommend this as a way of switching up your state.

Gratitude journalling

At the end of each day, write down the things that you are thankful for or appreciate. This can be as simple as one word or a longer explanation e.g., sunshine, a perfect avocado, a friend who listens to you without judgement or positive feedback at work. You can also extend this activity to include the reason for why you are grateful e.g., "I am grateful for my house as it helps me feel safe and secure and keeps me warm and dry".

Present: Increasing Positive Emotions

The more that you're present in what you are doing, the more you're able to experience pleasure. In a world where we are contactable 24/7 and have so many devices competing for our attention, it is worth looking at how you can be more mindful and in the moment. When I was writing this, I was looking at booking our summer holidays and I found an amazing range of French "glamping" sites. What drew me to them was the fact that there was no WiFi, which meant that the temptation to look at my phone and work would be completely removed, and I knew I would be able to be fully present with my family. I booked three weeks and I can't wait!

Alongside the growth in technology, meditation and mindfulness have increased in popularity over the last decade (in 2012, 4.1 per cent of people in the US reported using meditation; by 2017, it had increased to 14.2 per cent). People are seeking out ways to be more present with themselves and others, and meditation and mindfulness help to slow a busy mind.

You can develop your own mindful practice by:

- Setting clear intentions for what you are doing
- Reducing distractions
- Increasing awareness of your breathing
- Being aware of what is going on in your body
- Connecting to your senses
- Noticing the detail

You can tap into these feelings at mundane points in your day to cultivate a more mindful presence – for example, when you are doing the dishes, waiting in line or travelling on a bus or train. Put down your technology, and instead practise being present and aware of what's going on. This is something I have really struggled with and I have had to battle my phone addiction; phone and social media companies employ neuroscientists whose job it is to create dopamine tracks in apps and on devices so we use them more! Remember, they are plugging into the science I am talking about in this book to make sure you come back. It is something my friend Bret Freeman talks about in his TEDx talk entitled *Mind Control.*

In fact, this addiction to devices and the dopamine that you receive is something that psychiatrist Anna Lembke talks about in her book *Dopamine Nation.* Her advice is to go cold turkey and get rid of your phone for a month. She cites her own experience of doing this with teenagers struggling with anxious thoughts and depression and how in every case they felt better without their devices. I am not going to say get rid of your phones, but I propose that you start to consider your usage and your boundaries around it.

The simplest way to reduce the amount of time you spend on your phone is to put it in another room. James Clear, author and habit expert, calls this creating friction between an unhelpful habit and the frequency you do it. My phone is not in my office when I am working, not in my bedroom when I am sleeping and not in the room when I am watching a movie – these three things make a huge difference to my usage! Getting up to go into another room to use my phone seems crazy so I don't – that old adage out of sight, out of mind works. In a way, this is the opposite to value tagging where you put things that are important to you on vision boards or surround yourself with them; you're removing temptation and saying to your brain this isn't important.

Mindfulness is about experiencing all the feelings and learning to sit with both the negative and the positive ones. This helps you to tune in to what is going on for you and to understand where these feelings are coming from. This is the starting point of a practice and, like many of the exercises in this book, in order to feel the long-term benefits, you need to have done this over a period of time, averaging from one to three months. Consider how you can start to build this type of practice into your everyday life, as it has benefits beyond positive emotions by helping you to increase self-awareness and decrease stress.

Future: Visualization and Vision to Increase Positive Affect

Coaching is focused on your future state or desire. I work with clients to create a plan to go from where they are to where they want to be. They come to coaching because they are optimistic that the future holds promise, and I encourage you to feel the same. Optimism is defined by motivational speaker and author Simon Sineck as "the undying belief that the future is bright". The activities in this section will help you to tap into optimism and possibility.

What does visualization mean? Before we dive into the exercises, let's break down the word visualization. It can be off-putting as you may think you have to have perfect images in your head. It is estimated that 2–5 per cent of people can't see images in their mind's eye (I am one of them!) – this is called aphantasia and it can refer to a lack of ability to imagine any sensory experience.

If you struggle with seeing the image in your mind, vision boards and reflecting can be helpful. This is because by using vision boards you don't have to imagine the images, and reflections can be written or spoken, rather than needing visual representations.

Many people believe that their vision needs to look a certain way. This is no surprise given that we are conditioned to believe success means having a great job, a partner, 2–4 children and a beautiful house. This is such a narrow and limiting view, and doesn't fit everyone's aspirations – let's start with the fact that some women want a wife and not a husband, or don't believe in marriage, or simply want to be single, or don't want to have children. The list can go on!

In the words of Elsa, "let it go, let it go" – let go of what you think you "should" want. Your future vision may not look like your friend's, your mum's, that person you follow on Instagram's. It's yours. "Me too" aspirations can drive behaviour and quite frankly they do more harm than good, so promise yourself that you will quieten the inner voice saying, "You should have that" or "What about this?", or raising a rather curt eyebrow. It's *your* life and you only get one of them.

The exercises I'm going to share will help you to step into who you want to be, rather than who you are currently. Your identity isn't fixed and you can embrace a growth mindset and focus on what you want to change.

The science behind visualization: Visualization works because when you connect with and get super-clear on the future, you activate your PEAs – Positive Emotional Attractors – which work on three levels: through positive arousal, hormonal arousal and neurological activation. Richard Boyatzis, organizational behaviourist and psychologist, and his team at Case Western Reserve University in Ohio have studied both PEAs and NEAs (Negative Emotional Attractors) extensively to see which areas of the brain are impacted by them and what can trigger the negative or positive response. PEAs open up possibility, predominantly operating in the prefrontal cortex area of the brain. When these sites are activated, they trigger positive cognitive and physiological responses which link to enhanced motivation, creativity and resilience. When I work with clients who are in a funk, helping them tap into this big picture future and activating these PEAs can increase creativity and encourage engagement.

Equally, these activities help you to reduce stress and improve positive affect, enhancing your wellbeing, as in the PERMA model (see page 95). When you're in positive affect, it helps to reduce stress levels and calm the nervous system, meaning that you are cognitively better at making decisions, have enhanced memory and can think more clearly. Starting with vision and big-picture thinking is effective and it encourages engagement in coaching conversations, which means I often use it at the start to help frame a conversation and enable my clients to think positively. You will be exploring the steps to use visualization effectively later in this chapter. For now, let's look at the next stage of the PERMA model – engagement.

E – Engagement

Seligman describes this as "being at one with the music", which is similar to how the International Coaching Federation (ICF) describes presence or "dancing in the moment" with clients. Engagement means you're connected to and in tune with what's happening – for example, when you're focusing one thing rather than multitasking, or when you're really listening to the person who you are having a conversation with.

I think of engagement as being the opposite of multitasking, and mindfulness is a critical part of it. When you multitask, your brain's bandwidth is split. The prefrontal and dorsal frontal cortex areas of the brain have limited capacity so by multitasking, or effectively switching between tasks, your performance and cognitive abilities are diminished.[10] Instead, think about when you are so engrossed in an activity that you don't feel the need to respond to the multiple other demands on your attention – this is engagement!

Ask yourself what activities make you lose track of time? Do more of these! OK, it isn't always that simple, but you get the gist. Remember, these activities are likely to be the ones that play to your strengths, those you listed back in Step One when you were looking at what you enjoyed (see page 19).

To increase your engagement levels, you can:

- Practise mindfulness to connect with what you are doing and reduce distractions.
- Spend time in nature without any technology so you can be present to your surroundings. Tune in to what you notice and what you're feeling. Being in nature decreases stress, which in turn can give your brain more energy to focus on executive functions, such as problem-solving and decision-making. Going for walks is beneficial, both physically and cognitively, and is something that I do nearly every day.
- Get clear on your strengths and what you excel at. When you play to your strengths, you're more likely to be engaged.
- Do more of what you love: read about topics you find interesting, listen to podcasts and watch YouTube. Thinking about those topics you always want to learn more about is a great guide. These passions probably came up when you were looking at your values (see page 72). By following your internal compass, you will feel more engaged.

Equally, you can increase your engagement levels by focusing on the people around you and listening to them on a deeper level. The more that you listen to others and engage with them, the more effective your relationships will be because by really listening to others we are able to understand them more. Listening is one of the core coaching skills that I work with people to develop. There are three stages of listening:

Level 1: Listening in order to interject and add your point of view. I often call this queuing for talking and I can be particularly bad at this after a glass or two of wine, which isn't my most attractive trait!

Level 2: Listening to understand. You're more focused on the language and the congruence between body language, language and energy.

Level 3: Listening on the deepest level to what is and isn't being said and picking up on any subtle cues that there might be more going on.

Listening is a great way of making someone feel heard and seen. So much of our communication and conversations happen when there are other distractions, such as technology, around us. By practising your listening skills and being present, you are giving people your full attention. Listening to clients is a fundamental part of coaching and, as the second-fasted growing industry in the world, you can see that there is something special about being heard – so many people don't feel they are really listened to!

R – Relationships

When you're able to build positive relationships where you can communicate effectively and get your needs met, your wellbeing levels increase. There is evidence that strong relationships and support networks contribute to better physical health among older adults.[11]

Often, clients come to me because they are struggling in their relationships or feeling lonely. When I dig into what is going on, there may be several factors at play – for example, some clients feel that they have "grown apart" from romantic partnerships or friendships, whilst others feel that they want to have a romantic relationship. I support them to explore what's going on for them in terms of how they're feeling and thinking and help them move to a solution. This might be reconnecting with their old friends, starting new hobbies, developing existing friendships or extending their social circles. As many of my clients tend to work from home, this lack of connection with others can often be amplified.

Who is on your team?

This exercise, which I use with my clients, helps you to identify your feelings around your support network. It gives an audit of where you are in terms of your relationships and helps you identify what you need to change.

1. Draw a circle in the middle of a sheet of paper, then draw a circle around this and then a final outer circle, so you have three circles in total.

2. In the innermost circle, write down the people you could call in the middle of the night and you know they would be there – the people who you could rely on for everything. These might be family members or friends.

3. In the second circle, write down people you like and get on with. They might be workmates and more distant family and friends.

4. Finally, in the outer circle, write down those people who make your life a better place and support you, even though they may not even know! For example, the person you smile at on your morning run, the person who makes you coffee or the trainer in your gym class.

When you look at the circles, how do you feel? It isn't necessarily a good thing to have lots of people in your inner circle: if you have too many, you may feel stretched too thin. Equally if you don't have many people, consider who you may want to build and strengthen relationships with. Consider how you can do this so you feel more supported e.g., it may mean meeting new people or developing some of the relationships you already have. One way to do this might be through listening skills and being present, as explored on page 105. Being valued, seen and heard are at the core of building relationships.

M – Meaning or Purpose

I always think meaning and purpose are interchangeable words. Both are that sense that you are doing something which is bigger than you, that impacts the world in a positive way, improving your wellbeing.

You can increase your feelings of purpose by connecting with how you're supporting others, both in your working life and personal life. This can be as simple as spending time with others you care about, or on your passions and interests, or getting involved in voluntary work. Alternatively, it could be that your work or career gives you purpose as you can connect into the positive impact it is making.

Work is a big driver in my purpose. By training and teaching people to become coaches, I know that it's creating a massive ripple effect, where more people have access to quality coaching, enabling them to feel happier and more fulfilled. Equally, the relationships that I have with my immediate family and friends also give me meaning. Being able to emotionally support friends going through hard times, as well as celebrating the good times, makes me feel valued.

There is evidence that tapping into your purpose and being clear on where you're going can increase your life expectancy.[12] Looking at your purpose and living a life in congruence with it may help you to be happier, healthier and live longer. Of course, with anything, there are confounding variables. However, if you're on a mission to live a happier life, it makes sense to bring these practices into what you're doing. I believe that purpose and meaning correspond with the self-actualization part of Maslow's hierarchy of needs (see page 67); when you view these feelings through the lens that the supporting needs need to be met first, they will help you to move toward a more purposeful life.

A – Accomplishments

Acknowledging your part in your successes and celebrating your accomplishments activates the brain's reward centre, releasing dopamine. This can link back to gratitude, and having a daily or weekly practice of reflecting on what you've achieved. If you have a way of celebrating the quick, small wins, as well as the bigger goals and achievements, you are embedding a new process in your brain through neuroplasticity.

Another way of viewing accomplishments is to reframe the way that you look at goals. Often, performance is measured at a point in time and it is usually pretty black and white – you have either met the goal or you haven't. When you haven't met the goal, it can make you spiral into unhelpful negative thinking. As an alternative, you can look at mastery goal setting, where you look at what you want to accomplish in the long-term. Rather than measuring success at an arbitrary point in time, you are measuring and celebrating the progress you are making toward the goal. By switching up the way that you measure your success, you can build your feelings of accomplishment as you look at what you have achieved, rather than what you haven't.

Wellbeing and the PERMA model

I love using the PERMA model as it's a great way to identify what you're already doing well, alongside giving you some ideas about where you can focus. All this can help you feel better and enhance your wellbeing! It's also a great model to come back to as you can reassess where you are after making changes to a specific area. You may find that some of the areas you identified are similar to those in Step One: this is because different tools and lenses often reinforce where you need to focus. Equally, by using a variety of tools, you can start to find which you find most valuable and revisit those in the future.

REFLECTION

Journal using the following questions as prompts:

- What area of PERMA do you feel you are already doing well in?
- Where would you like to focus?
- What would success look like in this area?
- What are you going to commit to changing?
- How will you measure the success of these actions?

Research from the University College London shows it takes anywhere from 21–66+ days to form a habit, consider looking at this new action over three months to give yourself chance to implement the change and feel the benefits.

What do you want?

Now it's time to look at what you desire. You're going to tap into your inner creative child by doing a vision board or an action board. These work because, as neuroscientist Dr Tara Swart says, by looking at images on a vision board we are priming our brains to seek out opportunities which they may not have already noticed. Through the process of "value tagging", our brains hone in on what they think is important.

Of course, you can't create a vision board and sit back and expect everything to fall into place. The visual reminder needs to be in a place where you see it often; you need to reflect on it often and take regular action that aligns with it.

The process of getting creative can help to calm your nervous system and reduce your levels of stress and the associated neurotransmitters, including cortisol, which will allow you to access more of your executive functions.

Barbara Fredrickson, positive psychologist, developed the Broaden and Build Theory back in 1998. She says when you feel positive emotions, they help you to broaden your awareness, which opens you up to possibilities and means that you build on these over time. By broadening your perspectives and behaviour, you develop psychological resources which in turn means you think more effectively. Simply put, positive emotions and focusing on what you want helps you get there (you have to do the work too!).

Try the following exercises and activities to boost your focus on the positive.

The Be, Do, Have exercise

This can help you to connect with your desires before you do your vision board. It is one of my favourite coaching exercises, and I personally revisit it time and time again because it helps me reflect on where I am going.

As always, remember to lean into any feelings of resistance when you are doing this exercise and pay attention to your thoughts and emotions, writing them down as you go along.

Under each heading write down what you want to be, do or have in the future. I've included some examples:

Be	Do	Have
Happy	Less work	Regular holidays
Healthy		Beautiful house

Remember not to edit what you are writing – just be aware of your thoughts and feelings. You can be the biggest blocker to your progress, often, because you believe that certain things aren't possible for you. I have been there so many times when I struggle to articulate my goals or be honest about where I want to be because my inner critic is shouting "You are not good enough for this". Remember to swap those unhelpful thoughts for helpful ways of thinking.

When you have your completed list, it's time to cut it down – for each of the points write a sentence about why you want them e.g. "I want to be healthy as I want to live as long a life as I can", "I want regular holidays as they make memories and make me happy". If you can't articulate the reasons behind why you want something, then it is unlikely it is important to you.

Once you have an abridged list, reduce this further. Identify the order you want things, with the most important at the top and least important at the bottom. This will help guide what you put on the vision board and is the first step to your big vision.

The Best Possible Future Self exercise

This exercise is designed as a short, written visualization. In a meta-analysis of studies Heekerins and Eid from Freie University in Berlin, found that there was a positive increase in both positive affect and optimism after people had done this exercise, suggesting that it can increase levels of wellbeing and therefore happiness and contentment.[13]

1. Find somewhere quiet and get into a comfortable seated position. Ensure that your feet have contact with the ground.
2. Close your eyes or lower your gaze.
3. Focus on breathing into your belly with a longer exhale than inhale.
4. Now, imagine that you are at a future point in time where you have achieved the most important goal you have been working on. Take some time to feel into:
   - What you can see
   - What you can hear
   - What you can feel
   - Who is around you
   - How you are behaving
   - What you have achieved
   - Who you are being
5. Take some time to really appreciate where you are.
6. Come back to the present and slowly open your eyes and reconnect to the room around you.
7. In order to be this person, reflect on the following:
   a. What do you need to let go of right now?
   b. What do you need to do more of?
8. Make a commitment to start doing these things from this moment onwards.

I added in question 7 as I find it really powerful. When I do this exercise with clients, and they tune into what they need to get rid of to move forward, there are usually big "aha" moments. These are often mindset related: a lack of confidence, the belief that they can't move forward, their unhelpful thought patterns – and they begin to step into a feeling that change is possible and really commit to their goal. Equally, when they focus on what they want to do more of, it is more action-focused. I hope you had some "aha" moments when you reflected on these questions.

Like vision boards, this exercise helps to "value tag" what is possible for you and can be the foundation of building a new neural pathway, which you can strengthen with action and daily visualization.

After completing this exercise, ask yourself if this all makes sense given what you know and feel about yourself. This can add more inspiration for your vision board.

Making your vision board

The traditional way, and the way that I prefer, is to get a heap of magazines and newspapers, cut out images and words and stick them on a large piece of paper or card. Physically doing something can make you feel more engaged, which is positive for wellbeing. Making it into an arts and crafts type activity helps me connect with my inner child, who loved art and was super-creative, which enhances my positive emotions. If you have had a bad experience of art, or if you find doing it digitally works for you, then you can go ahead and do it that way.

When you are selecting images, consider:
- How you want to feel
- What you want to be doing
- What you want to be thinking
- What you want to have

Use what you learnt from the Be, Do, Have and Future Self exercises, to help to guide you.

I recommend that you go through your magazines or digital material in two ways:

1) Select the things that you want, the experiences you want, how you want to feel, what you want to be thinking and what you want to be doing. Cut out or print any images or words which represent these different categories.

2) Go through with a second lens, considering what resonates with you and what makes you feel the emotions you want to be feeling in the future.

When you have gathered everything, go back to your list and ask yourself what is missing and what you might want to add or take away. This is a further sense and reality check that helps you to connect emotionally with what you have compiled.

Finally, spread everything out on the card or paper. Consider how you position the images and words. The eye is drawn to the centre, so it might be that you put what is most important there. As this is going to become the visual manifestation of your vision, I recommend that the first stage is you pinning or BluTack-ing the images and words. Then come back and revisit with fresh eyes:

- How do you feel when you look at the board? (You want to be feeling inspired, motivated and excited.)
- What do you feel you need to move?
- What do you feel you need to add?

When you are happy with it, you can stick everything down. Put it somewhere that you will see it frequently. You could also take a photo of it to use as a screensaver on your phone or computer, so you are reminded of it again and again – the repetition helps to build those neural pathways.

An alternative way of doing this is to get a large corkboard and pin on the images and words. This is less permanent and you can update it as you move through the book and do more reflection. It may work better if your vision isn't super-clear right now, or if you are like me and tend to have your head turned by shiny objects and new things.

Finally, if you are more inclined to, set up a Pinterest board or use one of many vision board apps or programs to help support you. This may be better if you don't hold the love of craft that I do or are more digitally literate. Make sure that you use it as your screensaver and look at it regularly, as the danger with digital is that we can do it and then forget about it. As the physical vision board is somewhere prominent in your house, you can't miss it!

Building a visualization practice

Daily visualization can take many different forms. You could use your vision board as a prop to centre and ground your practice or you may wish to use the "my future self" exercise.

My personal visualization or "creative imagination" practice, as I like to call it, works like this: each year, usually in the first week of January, I create a vision board to give me a focus. Then, between three to five times a week, I do a visualization exercise like this:

- I close my eyes
- I imagine that I am at a future point in my life
- I connect in with what I am thinking, feeling and hearing

- I consider what and who is around me
- I spend some time breathing and tapping into my thoughts and emotions
- I bring myself back to the present
- I write down some key words

I have been doing this for so long that now it only takes a few minutes. Like most things, the little and often approach works for me. Often my visualization is on a specific feeling or thing, depending on what I feel I need. I am a huge fan of the 80 per cent rule as I find that this helps me stay on track with my goals more consistently than telling myself things need to happen every day. If I aim for daily and for whatever reason miss a day, it can put me into a spiral where I stop. Giving my brain the goal of 80 per cent means I don't go to that all or nothing place and I am more likely to stay committed to what I am doing. I encourage you to be flexible on the everyday narrative as well.

There is evidence that if you spend time each week connecting to that bigger vision, you are more likely to get there – that visualization practices can help you achieve your goals more successfully. In a study cited in The *Journal of Consulting Psychology* one group of job seekers received traditional career counselling and interview coaching; a second group also learned visualization techniques. Two months after the training, 66 per cent of those who were in the visualization group had new jobs compared to 21 per cent in the other group.

When you visualize or imagine that you are doing something, it stimulates the part of the brain that is responsible for the action. It is a tool that is often used by athletes, everyone from Usain Bolt to Jonny Wilkinson to Serena Williams are fans of and credit it as one of the practices that has helped them to achieve and succeed. It is the process of setting the intention, imagining that you have got there and then executing the plan. Olympian Jessica Ennis-Hill says, "I used visualization to think about the perfect technique. If I could get that perfect image in my head, it helped me channel my physical performance." This doesn't mean that solely by visualizing you will be successful, but the evidence that it helps increase the likelihood of success is compelling.

So, how do you tap into the benefits of visualization?

1) Get clear on what you want. Your vision board and Be, Do, Have findings will help with this. Be as specific as you can and take some time to imagine what success will look and feel like, tapping into the emotional, cognitive and physical sensations. You are effectively travelling to a future point in time and looking at what success is like there.

2) Each day revisit step one and spend time imagining you are there. You may be able to close your eyes and see where you want to be, or it might work for you to write it down or record a voice note on your phone. We can't all visualize or see images in our mind, which is why prompts such as vision boards are helpful.

3) Take action toward this future state every day, even if it is a tiny step.

This builds and strengthens neural pathways, which will be reinforced with daily action, priming your brain for success and supporting you to change.

Setting out the vision board allows you to create that deeper connection to yourself and your future desires. You are saying

"This is what I want and desire", programming the brain to know that it's important. It is like waving a flag to the brain to say "Hey this is key for me". As well as naturally seeking out opportunities to move toward the things which are important to you, you will realize it is OK to say no to things which won't move you toward the things on your vision board.

During lockdown in 2021, I ran a vision board workshop for my friends. A lot of us were struggling with our wellbeing so I thought it would be a fun thing to do and help us tap into positive affect (from PERMA), increasing our motivation. A close friend created a board that was a very different vision from where she was currently. It took her just under two years to get there and she is now happier than ever. This stuff works – and it works even better when we back it up with action!

KEY POINTS TO REMEMBER

- Connecting to your sense of purpose will improve your wellbeing.
- Visualization activates your PEAs (Positive Emotional Attractors).
- Having a clearer vision of what you want will guide how you behave.
- A vision board is an effective visual prompt of your desires.
- There is a clear link between a daily visualization practice and achieving goals.

5

Goal-setting and Focus

Now it is time to move from your big vision to specific goals and actions, which will strengthen your new neural pathways. The brain loves repetition; the more that neurons fire together, they wire together so your action reinforces your thinking. This is about creating a plan for what is next.

In this chapter, you will explore:

- Breaking down your vision into actionable goals
- How goal theory links to motivation
- Structuring your plan
- How the brain and neuroplasticity support change

SMART goals as a starting point

You may have heard of SMART goals, which work from the premise that you're more likely to achieve goals if they are:

- Specific
- Measurable
- Achievable

- Realistic
- Time bound

When I work with clients who have struggled with goal-setting, I use this simple SMART formula to help them focus on and sense check their goals so they are more meaningful.

Specific

When we were thinking about moving house, it was really important to me to be close to the forest. When I pictured the house that I wanted to live in, it was less than five minutes' walk to the forest and I imagined taking a coffee there on my morning walks. The house we now live in is opposite the forest and I go for a morning walk most days, often with a coffee. The specificity helped me to narrow down what I wanted and it acted as a sorting mechanism when we were house-hunting. By getting to the specific desire, we were able to take action to get to where we are now.

Measurable

Ensuring our goals are measurable is the foundation of coaching conversations. Without a measure of success, we can't see progress. The focus gives direction. You need to be able to measure what you are doing to assess what is and isn't working. I am a big fan of a data-driven approach. This doesn't only mean spreadsheets (I actually hate spreadsheets) – it is also important to assess how you feel.

I will be sharing how to measure and the self-determined scales you can use, which build on the Wheel of Life exercise (see page 8). Remember, this is your starting point and has determined your current focus – if that has changed since you first did the exercise, you can revisit it. Nothing is set in stone.

Achievable and realistic

Goals that are too big and too far away from your current reality will be overwhelming and demotivating. You need smaller "wins", which is why having targets can help – for example, if you have never run before, your big goal may be to run a marathon one day but your initial goal might be to run 5km. As much as I am unlikely to win the 100m at the Olympics, I am also unlikely to suddenly become a billionaire overnight. The reason that you looked at where you are first is to contextualize your goals and give them some grounding. As you move toward your bigger goal and start to achieve and celebrate milestones, you can open up your thinking to even bigger possibilities. You are the one who decides what you can achieve.

Breaking your dream down into manageable chunks works – for example, I had a client who dreamt of being a Hollywood actor. Whilst we worked together, she broke this down into more specific goals: being in a film, which would be shown at a specific film festival, and winning a role in a TV series. She achieved these goals and is now working toward her dream step by step. I am looking forward to seeing her on the big screen in the future!

Some people argue that setting achievable and realistic goals is limiting. However, I would argue that you are contextualizing your path to success. As someone who has dipped her toes into the world of energetics and is a certified energy coach, I think we need to treat "quantum leaping" with caution. This is the idea you can transcend normal timelines and therefore what doesn't seem possible given your context today can seem possible tomorrow.

When people talk about quantum leaping, they refer to what is known in physics as a quantum jump, where an electron in an atom jumps from one energy level to another. There is no in-between state. Researchers at Yale University saw that this was a possibility – for example, a student might "quantum leap" from failing to being top of the class. Now, there are examples of this happening with what appears to be no transition between the states. In the world of energetic coaching, people talk about leaps or jumps where people seem to change their state or magnetism instantly and make huge life changes in incredibly short timelines.

In the work I have done, and the people I have spent time with, I've found that success which appears like a leap has been grounded in a lot of previous work. The old saying "It took me 20 years to be an overnight success" is true. Often, the compound effect of doing a lot of work over years can lead to growth, which feels like it is accelerated – for example, clients who have been building businesses for years hit a certain income level and then seem to "leap" to the next level in a short period of time. Although from the outside, this seems like a leap it can be attributed to the work they have put in before.

In its second year, the growth of my training business looked exponential from the outside – we increased our revenue by nearly ten times. This was partly because I had an existing business and a reputation in the field, and partly because we were tapping into a growing market. Of course, there were elements of risk taking, and the fact that my team and I worked hard and put customer experience at the heart of what we did. There was also luck and a lot of learning (aka mistakes). I remember saying to my coach, "I don't ever want another year at this intensity!". What helped me with the growth was the fact that I believed it was possible and, energetically, I was tuned into the fact that I could make a leap from where we were to where we wanted to be. This is the most direct way that I can see the theory of quantum leaping applying to our development or our progress; if we believe it is possible to accelerate our progress and decrease timelines, our brains will seek out opportunities which help make it a possibility.

In fact, that experience led me to take a different strategy in our third year. We focused on consolidation, systems and processes for the next "leap", building on my previous comment that the compound effect of effort between the leaps is often what powers that "sprint" or period of acceleration. From year two to three, we maintained our revenue and solidified our position, ready for the next burst of growth. This links into the growth cycle and the fact that growth is rarely linear; it is normal to have periods where you flatline, or even go backwards, before you go forwards again.

Significant change is possible when you feel aligned and present with what you're doing (the engagement piece of PERMA – see page 95). I am pretty much living proof of this. I was dismissed by so many people (mainly myself) in my 20s and 30s and continue to be so even now, yet I always come back fighting, happier, healthier and wealthier than I have ever been.Contextual factors *do* play a role in growth. However, my philosophy focuses on slow and steady consistent gains, which is looked at more in The Habits Academy, run by James Clear, author and habit expert. The compound effect of making small changes over time is extremely significant.

The thing about success and celebrating those achievements is that it starts to have a snowball effect. The more you achieve and celebrate, the better you feel (the A in PERMA). Equally, when you celebrate and acknowledge what you have done to achieve your goals, it helps to reduce imposter feelings, which come from attributing your success to external factors like luck, rather than internal factors such as hard work. If you take credit for what you have achieved, you are more likely to feel confident about achieving more. Building on feelings, thoughts and emotions in a positive way is how we develop new beliefs and ways of thinking through strengthening the neural pathways in the brain.

Time bound

Setting a date by which you want to achieve your goals helps to keep you accountable. When I have a fitness goal with a date attached, like a 10k run, it allows me to plan what I will do each week and put in milestones – these help me review where I am in relation to my goal and to celebrate those small steps, which is good for my wellbeing. I learnt about time the hard way; I did about six weeks training for the London Marathon because I got my place late in the day, and then the school I was working in went into special measures. I completely neglected to train and can still feel the pain in my calves when I think about it now. Having a plan is a good thing!

Building on SMART goal-setting

I work with some people who turn a shade of green when we talk about planning, and it's true that some of us are much more likely to plan than others. It isn't something which comes naturally to me; I prefer go with the flow or wing it. But I acknowledge that for some having a plan and a structure makes things easier.

Plans give you structure and enable you to execute your goals. Deadlines help keep you accountable. Breaking down big-picture thinking into smaller chunks can help you to achieve your goals and feel good along the way. Going back to the sporting analogy, if you want to get fit and run a 10km race, day one may be as simple as buying a running kit.

As the saying goes, "Rome wasn't built in a day". When we are looking at behavioural change, it is about building the foundations so that it is sustainable.

From a vision to goals

Using your vision board, and the findings of your Be, Do, Have and Future Self visualization exercises, now is the time to write down your vision statement. This could be a paragraph summarizing what is on your vision board, or if you can condense it into a sentence go ahead and do so!

Now you have this summary alongside your vision board, it is time to break it down into goals. A goal is the future desired state. Some people may struggle with the language of goals. As we learnt in DISC personality profiling (see page 50), only about 25 per cent of people are motivated by goals, but most of us are motivated by wanting things to change. If the term "goals" doesn't work for you, think about what you might call them instead – perhaps desires, points of focus, success factors!

It doesn't matter what you call them, they are the way of making your big vision tangible.

Goal-setting

Questions to answer:
- What do I want to achieve?
- What is my current main focus?

Now write down your list of goals from most important to least important.

Next, consider how these goals connect with your values and what is important to you. Go back to your list of values from Step One (see page 73) and look at them against the goals you have written down.
- How congruent are they?

Next, put your goals into categories. I've included some of my own examples:

My long-term goals are ones that I want to achieve in 1+ years:
- Paying off at least 20 per cent of my mortgage so we have more flexibility and security.
- Competing in a half marathon in October 2023, which will support my goal of health and wellbeing.

My medium-term goals are the ones I want to achieve in 6–12 months. They include:
- Investing in some house renovations, including updating our garden and garden office.
- Completing a 10k run in under an hour in January 2023.

My short-term goals are the ones I want to achieve in less than six months. They include:

- Running at least twice a week for 30 minutes at a time.
- Saving at least £1,000 a month.

Your short-term goals feed into your medium-term goals and then into your-long term goals. If they don't fit together like this, start with the long-term goals and work backwards. For example, if your goal is to get a promotion in a year what do you need to do? Examples might be:

- Have a conversation with your boss around targets.
- Seek out a mentor to support with your development.
- Create your own development plan so you can show evidence of success.
- Volunteer for a new area of work so you can boost your CV.
- Consider what activities have the biggest impact in your work.

When you have broken the goal down like this, allocate each step into the short-, medium- or long-term so you can then build your plan.

Goal theory and motivation

You have to be motivated to achieve your goals. There are two main types of motivation:

- **Intrinsic motivation:** You are motivated by the task itself.
- **Extrinsic motivation:** You are motivated by external factors.

Knowing where your motivation and drive comes from can help you to stay committed to your goals. Often your primary motivation or drive is to meet your basic needs: security and safety score highly here, which is why people step into one of four behaviours: fight, flight, freeze or fawn (see page 3) as nervous system responses.

Fight: You might fight or hustle to ensure these basic needs are met – working long hours or multiple jobs to make ends meet. Often this behaviour is ingrained so, years later when you don't need to work such long hours, it is your default and it's hard to unlearn! This was my default for years. When I feel that external pressure and threat to my safety or security, I work harder. It is why from the age of 18 I have had two jobs and spent most of my working life having some kind of side hustle. It took me a lot of work to realize this was a nervous system response and it was "safe" for me to take the foot off the gas sometimes!

Flight: You might also flee, which means you may not stick to one thing. You might find it hard to focus, leave jobs or give up on things. This is not you being lazy; it is a nervous system response to feeling overwhelmed. If this sounds familiar, remember this and be compassionate to your past self.

Freeze: You may freeze and do nothing. An example of this would be people who never open bank statements or answer the phone. Logically, they know facing up to what is going on makes sense but, because their nervous system is overstimulated, logic goes out of the window. I know I have, at times, felt like I am rooted to the spot and haven't acted due to being overwhelmed. I can now recognize this feeling, so I work hard to relax my nervous system in order to make decisions and think more clearly. My failsafe methods are walking in the forest, leaving technology behind or going to the sauna.

Fawn: You may fawn as a response which is a way to avoid conflict. It's a way of avoiding the threat by keeping the person threatening you happy – for example, your boss may say that your work isn't good enough in a meeting. Rather than having a confrontation, you accept what they say. I know I can do this at times to "keep the peace" and avoid conflict, especially with family. If this sounds familiar, consider how you can respond in a way which acknowledges the threatening behaviour without being confrontational.

If you feel that your basic needs are under threat, any of these behaviours can occur. It is why I recommend making a plan and getting support if needed, or it's going to be hard to move toward your goals – you'll be stuck in your nervous system response. Think about what needs to be in place for those basic needs to be met – for example, for you to pay your bills. When you have this figured out, and a way of meeting it, you can calm your nervous system and start to focus on bigger goals.

When your basic needs are met, your motivators change and you can look at your medium-term and long-term goals. This is when you start to consider whether what you are doing is congruent with your values. You may choose to seek out activities that give you that level of intrinsic motivation and value rather than those that offer an external reward: aka those activities where you feel really engaged. For most of us, both intrinsic and extrinsic motivation are at play in most situations – for example, you might choose your job because it pays your wages, but also because you find it interesting and rewarding too.

I often work with clients who struggle to get the balance right. One was an accountant with a well-known organization and, although she got paid well, she wasn't interested in the work. Over time, her motivation dipped as the extrinsic reward was no longer sufficient to keep her motivated. I helped her to explore her values and her intrinsic motivators, which included having a keen interest in developing others. She moved to a smaller firm where her role had a larger element of mentoring and leadership, enabling her to be more engaged in what she was doing.

The important takeaway is to always consider what is motivating you in any situation. Sometimes, when you find things boring, you may need external motivators and rewards to keep going. Equally, you might sometimes be motivated because you want to avoid negative external effects – for example, you complete your tax returns or pay parking fines as you don't want the negative consequences that will occur if you don't. These activities aren't pleasurable, but they help us avoid pain.

Remember, when you are serious about these goals, you have to consider what resources you need to ensure that they happen and how you will celebrate your accomplishments.

It is time to revisit where you are now and look at changing some of your thoughts, beliefs and emotions. I will be talking you through exercises which I use both myself and with my clients. Over time, you will be working with your neural pathways to change the wiring of your brain; remember neurons that fire together, wire together!

REFLECTION

Imagine that you've achieved these goals and consider:
- What do I need to do more of?
- What do I need to stop doing?

If you adopt the identity of someone who has achieved the success with these goals, start to tap into who you need to be.
- What is that person like?
- What do they think?
- What do they feel about themselves?

Re-programming your thinking

In Step One, we looked at identifying the unhelpful thoughts that you hold and replacing them with more helpful ways of thinking to support you in achieving your goals.

The language you use can have a significant impact on the way that you think. A simple way of looking at this is to read these sentences out loud and tap into how each one makes you feel on a physiological basis in your body and what it makes you think:

- I can't achieve my goal
- I can achieve my goal
- I will achieve my goal
- I am achieving my goal

By changing the prefix, we change the intention of our language and therefore pre-progam our neural pathways to believe that we are capable.

Lifelong learning has a positive impact on wellbeing.[14] By adopting this mindset and being open to formal and informal ways of learning, we can hypothesize that you will begin to feel better about yourself. Then, when you have a more positive self-image, you are more likely to achieve. One of my favourite Masters qualification modules, back in 2009, was on lifelong learning and the ability that everyone has to build new neural connections. This has stuck with me and is something that I embody in my work and in my relationships: everyone has the ability to change and to learn new things. How much do you commit to learning for life?

When I was working with a mentor on my Master Coach accreditation, my coaching sessions were recorded and assessed against a set of competencies. I recorded a session and submitted it as a starting point. The first feedback I received was pretty dreadful, but I remember saying to my mentor, "I have a growth mindset so starting here doesn't matter – I can get better". He smiled. A year later, I had my accreditation and am now one of fewer than 70 Master Coaches in the UK at the time of writing. If I didn't have this mindset, I don't think I would be where I am today. This kind of thinking is the big divider between those who don't and those who do; believing that you can starts with those thoughts. Continue your brain diet with optimism, and with learning from what you have achieved and what has gone before.

Building new beliefs

Our beliefs are the assumptions and thoughts we hold about what we can or can't do and they act as a sieve in our brains, where we filter out what isn't consistent with the belief. Therefore, over time, they become more and more ingrained.

Our beliefs matter because they can hold us back from doing what we want to do, which is why they are often called "limiting beliefs".

When I work with clients, I often see beliefs layered on top of each other. They are generally formed during childhood when we are learning to make sense of the world and there is often an underlying belief of "not being good enough" or "not being enough". We add many other layers of beliefs on top and our brain unconsciously filters out things which are not congruent with these.

Many people will share that there are times when they have not felt good enough and it has stopped them from moving forward. I've experienced this too. I would say that the "not good enough" voice is nowhere near as loud as it has been in the past but when I am stepping out of my comfort zone, or I am being more visible, I still hear it. I know I am not alone; even Beyoncé is reported to have fears and feelings of not been good enough! This is part of how your brain keeps you safe, but you can turn the volume down too!

You can't wave a magic wand and suddenly go from not feeling good enough to feeling good enough. Instead, it is about digging into the origin of the belief and building a new neural pathway and way of being which is congruent with being good enough. This takes time, energy and motivation.

Neuroplasticity in action

The aim is to effectively plough a new pathway in your brain. Imagine that you are trying to cross a field with high grass, poppies and thistles – you scan your way through and notice a well-trodden path. That is the route you take. And this is really how our brain works – going down that well-trodden route again and again. When you are building a new neural pathway and creating a new belief or way of being, you have to walk through the long grasses and brambles. At first, it can be really hard – you will feel resistance and it will take a lot of energy and focus to get through. Over time, the more you go down this route, the easier it becomes. At the same time, if you stop using the other path it starts to grow over and becomes harder to use.

This is how our beliefs work – they are based on neural pathways and we need to execute a new one and build it up through motivation and focus to ensure that we can achieve the change we desire. Remember, your beliefs unconsciously govern your behaviour and therefore your ability to achieve your goals, so this work needs to be done alongside the actions you are taking to achieve your goals.

Believing you are good enough

Imagine that you believe you are good enough to achieve whatever you want to achieve – you are a 10/10 on your belief.
- What would you be thinking?
- What would you be feeling?
- How would you be interacting with others?

- How would you be showing up each day?
- What would you be doing more of?
- What would you be doing less of?

You might want to revisit the Future Self visualization (see page 112) at this point to focus on you being the best that you can be and believing that everything you want is possible. Hopefully, you have been practising this visualization regularly!

The visualization helps to build the neural pathways, but to embed these and strengthen them you need to back it up with action. You need to do something to secure the change in the brain and the deeper behavioural change. Start to think about:

- What small action you can take every day to help move me toward this future place
- When you will take the action
- How you will celebrate doing this

For example, when you are a 10/10 on confidence and belief, you might be presenting to a room of 1,000 people. What is the first step to getting there? It could be watching a TED talk by someone you think is a great presenter and noticing the behaviours that they exhibit. It could be speaking up in a meeting rather than staying quiet. It could be enrolling onto a public speaking course. The most important thing is that you are starting to take small steps toward the desired future state. And that is how it works: small steps over time equal big results!

This methodology of building new beliefs rather than working to eradicate old beliefs is supported by growth mindset and neuroplasticity. I personally don't buy into this idea that we can quickly swoosh away old beliefs because they are embedded in our neural pathways, so unless something significant happens in our brain our best chance is to create a new way of thinking and reinforce its meaning. Over time, the old pathways will become weaker and eventually die out. Again, this is part of my whole approach to change: sustained, slow and consistent and it is the science behind how coaching works, which is why so many of my clients return to me years later to share how they are still feeling the benefits of coaching.

KEY POINTS TO REMEMBER

- Make sure your goals are SMART.
- It is possible to re-program your thinking and build new beliefs.
- Visualization and action need to work together to support lasting change.

6

Stepping into Your
New Identity

Planning is a way of working with the brain to further deepen your new neural connections. When you start to think about how you will do things, you are laying the groundwork for those things to start happening and making possibilities more probable. It is about setting the conditions for success, so that you can move forward with purpose and direction and enhance your probability of succeeding.

In this chapter you will explore:

- Success habits
- Creating morning and evening routines
- Planning for energy and performance
- How to keep yourself accountable and focused
- The 80/20 rule and ensuring that you stay 'on track'

Your success habits

I think of success habits as the things that you do for yourself knowing that they will help you to meet your goals and be more successful in all areas of your life. They are probably a lot of the things you already know in terms of traditional wellbeing like getting enough sleep, drinking water and eating green vegetables; you know the drill!

Success habits are the things that are helpful for you if you have them in place most of the time. "The way you do one thing is the way you do everything." What does this mean? If you show up for yourself, then this impacts how you do everything.

I am not one of the gurus who says you should not do X, Y and Z. Yes, we know that science says that you are likely to function more effectively cognitively if you "eat the rainbow", but this doesn't mean that if you have McDonalds for tea and drink wine you won't be successful. I have experienced for myself, and seen with clients, that when we label things as good or bad and we fall off the good wagon, we really fall off.

Success leaves clues and it is true that those who are most successful and determined often display different characteristics and behaviours to those who aren't. In fact, psychologist Angela Duckworth came up with a measure that was directly related to performance known as "grit", which measures the extent to which you stay focused on and committed to your goals.

So, how do some people stay on track and gritty whilst others don't? Often, it may be linked to this concept of growth mindset, where people connect with their ability to improve and learn.

Equally, it may be down to people's goal focus. We know from personality theory that some people tend to have a preference for goals and therefore may be at an advantage for grittiness. However, we equally know that if we are incentivized and believe we can achieve, we are more likely to do so.

The power of sleep

When we stop prioritizing ourselves and our self-care everything else becomes a bit harder. When I work with clients, especially high-performing leaders and business owners, we often end up looking at their sleep. This is because quality and quantity of sleep has a direct impact on performance at work. When people are stressed or are overloaded, their sleep often suffers, which can have knock-on effects on their wellbeing. I explore this with clients through self-report questionnaires and by listening and responding to what they share. This is usually the starting point of understanding the root cause of their sleep difficulties, which is usually stress caused by work, finances, relationships or health (or a combination of all four). Through coaching, I support my clients to identify the stressors and create a way forward to decrease their intensity, or develop coping mechanisms that help them to deal with the stressors more effectively.

Simply put, if you are not getting sufficient sleep it has an impact on your cognitive processes such as your memory[15] and your cognitive performance.[16] A lack of sleep means that you are not as good as you could be, something we have all probably experienced. Alongside a reduction in performance, sleep deprivation is also linked to more emotional responses, especially around anger[17] and an amplification of emotions.[18] If we don't sleep enough, our emotional intelligence is reduced and we are more likely to react rather than respond.

I know I have experienced this many times over. I remember only too well being at work after late night partying in my 20s, or a sleepless night with my kids in my 30s and not being able to focus on what I was doing. Even now, when I don't get a good night's sleep, I feel slower and I know that I need to give myself some TLC rather than "push through" or make big decisions.

There is a clear link between stress and sleep, with stress and chronic cortisol exposure decreasing quality of sleep and then, in turn, this lack of sleep increasing stress levels, and round it goes. You need an intervention to break this cycle, usually by reducing stress levels.

In the UK and US, people are sleeping less. A survey by Direct Line insurance company in 2022 found that 14 per cent of adults in the UK sleep less than five hours a night and 71 per cent of adults don't have the recommended seven to nine hours sleep per night. Of those surveyed, 34 per cent said their poor mental and physical health was impacted by a lack of sleep.

You probably have got the message: sleep is essential for you to operate at an optimum level. If you are a new parent, remember that this period will pass so maybe come back to this section. If you have a sleep disorder, seek medical support. For everyone else reading this, it's time to up your sleep hygiene.

This is going to be the one thing that makes the biggest difference to your wellbeing, so aim for a sleep schedule that you can follow consistently. This is certainly not one of those books that advises you to get up at 5am each morning, although if this works for you and you don't mind a 9–9.30pm bedtime, then go right ahead.

Sleep hygiene

Work out how much sleep you need: for most people it is seven to eight hours a night. Keep a sleep diary and see how you feel after different amounts of sleep. Then, it is about giving yourself the best conditions for sleep. Making your bedroom an inviting place to sleep helps. The purpose is to set an intentional space for you to sleep:

- Make sure your bedroom is dark and peaceful, without distractions.
- Reduce exposure to blue light from devices, at least 30 minutes before bedtime.
- Take all devices out of your room.
- Have a wind-down routine, which may include having a bath, journalling, reading, meditating, speaking to your partner or stretching.

Ideally, avoid consuming alcohol and caffeine before bedtime and give yourself a couple of hours after eating before you go to sleep. Remember my 80/20 rule here and please don't think that a couple of nights of having coffee or a glass of wine or whisky will derail you. This is about finding your rhythm the majority of the time.

One of my favourite ways to unwind before bed is to go to the spa for an hour at 8.30pm and then, go straight to bed when I get home. I also find swimming helps me to calm my nervous system. One day, I might have my own swimming pool (one for the vision board), which would be more calming than driving to the gym and back to use one! On evenings I don't go to the gym, I like to have a bath or do some gentle stretching or have a chat with my husband.

I equally know what really doesn't work; taking my laptop to bed to catch up on work, watching something or looking at my phone before bedtime. I don't know if it is the blue light or the fact that it is work, but I never sleep well after doing this. Eating too close to bedtime always makes me feel wide awake and drinking a lot of alcohol affects my sleep too, and gone are the days of crawling into bed after midnight. Well, nearly gone!

It's true that a successful morning routine is based on an established and consistent evening routine so set this up in a way that will work for you. The easiest way to set your "bedtime" is to look at when you need to get up, and work back 8–8.5 hours. My earliest possible wake-up time is 6am, so I am usually in bed by 10pm. When I train at our academy in the evenings, I always have a lie-in the next day as find I am buzzing from being around the students so need some time to unwind and switch off my brain.

These are all things that work for me – what works for you may be different. I am blessed with two children who are more night owls than larks, so the early morning gives me some time on my own. I am usually awake before anyone else in my house has stirred, not quite at 5am, although as I am getting older it seems like sometimes my body naturally wakes at this time. When it does, I embrace it although I do sometimes need a power nap during the day.

REFLECTION

Journal your answers to the questions below, so you can then translate the answers into an actionable plan. Remember that this is a process: if your sleep is awful right now, it might be that you look at changing one element of your evening routine to start working with your brain's plasticity to build new habits.

- How would you describe your current sleep patterns?
- What are the areas you would like to focus on?

- What will you do to increase your sleep quality?
- What can you do to ensure you get enough sleep?
- How will you monitor your sleep patterns moving forward?
- What are the steps that you are going to take to improve your sleep?

Morning routine

As with everything else in life, effective and successful morning routines start with planning. When you have worked out what time you will wake up, you might want to consider what your routine looks like.

I remember listening to a podcast about the morning routines of successful people and one of them involved hanging upside down for 30 minutes like a bat. I am still quite transfixed as to what equipment this would need and how you would feel doing this. This isn't the kind of routine I am going to suggest, although if you do try it can you send me a photo?

In his book *The Miracle Morning*, Hal Elrod created a craze for morning routines which seem to be anything from Mark Wahlberg's 2.30am wake-up call for prayer and a workout to Jeff Bezos's no meetings before 10am rule and a routine which involves coffee, papers and breakfast with his kids, as well as "pottering". Then there is Sara Blakely, founder of Spanx, who starts her day with yoga before making breakfast for her kids and taking them to school, and Arianna Huffington, who chooses to wake naturally and meditate.

Your circumstances will, in part, determine your routine so consider the ingredients you want to include. Many people swear by exercising first thing, as it "sets you up for the day". It can ensure that your body is oxygenated and help to provide clarity and focus. Exercise may be walking the dog, doing some yoga or a more energetic and upbeat activity. You need to consider what works best for you.

If exercise first thing doesn't work, it might be that you have tea or coffee and some time to reflect and reset either with meditation, journalling or sitting in silence. Again, this is your choice and like everything the best thing to do is to start small, test, collect your data (which can be your emotions) and then repeat or revise.

Rather than establishing a 10-step plan, consider one or two things that would make a difference to you in the morning. I find it is often what I don't do rather than what I do – for example, by staying away from my phone and social media until after the school run, I find I can be more focused and more present. I also find some kind of movement is energizing. I am lucky that my Pilates teacher, Natalie Grace, lives round the corner from me and, as she is also a friend, I would never miss our 7am twice-weekly appointments. The same is said of when I run with my two friends in the morning. Accountability does work! (A shoutout to my running buddies, Sonja and another Natalie.)

REFLECTION

- What is your morning routine?
- What do you need to add in?
- What will you take away?

Exercise

As well as the benefits to our physical and mental health, exercise can help us function more efficiently cognitively – enabling us to make better decisions, be more focused and build new neural pathways more effectively.

The key to exercising regularly is finding something that you enjoy as the positive emotional response will release dopamine. This helps to reinforce the behaviour, so you are more likely to repeat it. If you don't experience pleasure doing something, it is less likely you will want to repeat the behaviour.

I find that I go in cycles. I have become a bit of a Pilates addict and I fall in and out of favour with HIIT training, cycling, running, walking and swimming. I now do what I feel like doing and ask myself: what would feel good today? As long as I move, I don't think it makes that much difference whether I am swimming or jumping! For years, I thought exercise had to be a certain way and I was doing it to look good rather than to feel good. Now, I prioritize the latter and it means I am much more likely to commit to daily exercise. I'm happy if I achieve 80 per cent of my exercise goal – my own benchmark.

One of the reasons I think the 80 per cent rule works is it gives me leeway. When I slip below 60 per cent, which is exercising four out of seven days a week, it is a flag to me to look at what is going on. It usually means I am getting complacent about my behaviour, I don't have a clear goal or I have too much going on and feel overwhelmed. Being able to see the change in behaviour is always a sign I need to do something different.

Questions to consider when exploring what exercise to do:
- What exercise have you enjoyed in the past?
- What do you really not enjoy?

- What have you been curious about trying?
- What exercise options would you like to test over the next month?
- When will you schedule in your time?
- How will you measure your enjoyment levels?

Meditation and mindfulness

The benefits of meditation and mindfulness practices are that they reduce stress levels, which has a positive impact on brain health. Equally, they can enable us to be more present, which can improve our focus, energy and flow state.

I know that meditation rewires your brain, reduces stress, enhances thinking and is amazing for you cognitively. However, I don't do it! I have never found it enjoyable and whenever I start a meditation practice, I feel an immense amount of resistance to the extent that I start doing things like cleaning rather than meditating. For years, I felt like this was my guilty secret in the personal development world because I know how beneficial meditation is!

Although I don't meditate, I do lie down after yoga (I used to find this so hard and wanted to jump up and scream, so I have made some progress), I walk or run in nature and swim. I also find sitting in the sauna strangely meditative and can completely zone out. However, if someone *tells* me to zone out, it doesn't work for me.

I share this because often you can be told something is amazing for you and that you really must do it, and it just doesn't work for you. We are all unique so, when you are reading this book, focus on the things that work for you, rather than the things that don't. This is your permission slip to give things a go and then if they don't feel good, decide to park them. Your life. Your rules. Everything in this book is backed up by evidence so, if you do implement it, it will work. Equally, you don't have to do everything!

Planning for energy and performance

Our energy levels and how we feel impacts how we show up and the effort that we put into things. We aren't designed to be "doing" the whole time; we need to alternate that with periods of "being".

Reflect on when you feel most energetic and what you need to have in place to feel this way. The way that you show up will impact the end result, so if you are aware you aren't feeling on top form consider how you can change your state before you take on a task, such as attending an important meeting, writing, doing some research or even having an awkward conversation.

Understanding your individual energy needs makes a difference to how you structure your time. Start to look at when you are feeling excited and engaged and when you are not, and the ingredients that are there in each case. Consider how to map out what you can do to transition between different activities and energetic states. Keep in mind that if you are a woman, your energy levels and overall state may be affected by which point you are at in your menstrual cycle.

When I trained as an energy coach, one of the most important things that we focused on was how we were feeling and what we could do to get into the right state to support our clients. Our state dictates our energy, so if I am feeling a bit down or low in energy when I am teaching or training, I am not as magnetic to others as if I am feeling upbeat and positive. That is why I have a ritual before I get in the virtual or physical classroom, which can either include some breathing exercses, power poses or dancing to switch up how I feel. The way that you present yourself will impact how others respond.

Energy and chakras

Chakras (see page 21) are energy points in the body that are used in yoga and meditation. There is evidence that these energy points are responsible for different feelings and emotional states. When you move from the base of your spine up to the top of your head, each energy point relates to a different core emotion from guilt and shame up to purpose and love. In energy work we believe that you are always vibrating at a certain frequency related to the emotion that you are feeling and embodying. When you become magnetic, which is where people want to be around you, you're at your highest vibration which is the frequency of love.

Body scan

A great way to connect with your chakras is to do a body scan:

1) Make sure you are sitting comfortably and have your feet flat on the floor.
2) If you want to, close your eyes or lower your gaze.
3) Take a few deep breaths, feeling the air travel all the way down through your body.
4) Connect with the soles of your feet on the floor and, as you breathe, gradually scan up your body: your shins, knees, thighs, buttocks, lower back, stomach and solar plexus (this is an area of nerves at the bottom of your

stomach), chest, shoulders, neck, chin, mouth, cheeks, eyes, third eye (in the middle of your forehead slightly above the gap between your eyebrows) to the top of your head – your crown.

5) Notice what each area feels like and where you feel any resistance or discomfort.

6) When you get to the top of your head, or your crown, imagine that there is a white beam of light going from there up into the sun.

7) Take some time to feel that light emitting through your body.

This exercise helps you connect to your chakras, especially your crown chakra at the top of your head, which can raise your vibration energetically.

On a basic level, this is about looking at how you can raise your vibration and feel better. If you are feeling stuck in guilt, shame, anger, frustration or resentment, it is important that you not only sit with the emotion but that you can then move on to a more positive emotion.

When I talk about sitting with the emotion, it is about feeling it and being present with it. Often, when I am feeling something negative, I do my best to distract myself as the feeling is uncomfortable. However, when I don't sit with it, I don't process it. Sitting with it is acknowledging the feelings and emotions and what might have caused them. It is about allowing yourself to feel sad or angry and to cry if you need to (or shout or scream). I have always believed that letting emotions out is healthy and that if we don't, it can lead to complications down the line. Someone told me a few years ago that when we cry our tears contain cortisol, so crying helps you to get rid of stress! I remember this when I cry.

When you allow yourself to feel and process the emotions, remember that it might make you feel worse before you feel better. Practise self-care and, if you need to, seek additional support from a friend, family member or seek external support from a counsellor or therapist.

We know, cognitively, that positive emotions and positive affect impact our thinking and creativity; on an energetic level, they impact how we show up and respond to others.

Reflect on what you really need to feel energized and focused, and how you can change your state if you are feeling stuck or overwhelmed. I encourage you to start to build up a toolkit of activities which help you to feel good, perhaps dancing, listening to music and practising gratitude (see page 97).

Personal accountability and responsibility

One of the things that I've noticed makes the biggest difference to my clients is the extent to which they take personal responsibility for their actions. When they take on full ownership and responsibility, they often achieve more. This doesn't mean that they always get it right. In fact, part of the work is about reflecting on when things haven't worked out and what they would do differently as a result, which helps embed learning and allows people to move forward.

These are your goals and your vision. How committed are you to them?

We all come from different backgrounds and have differing resources. I want you to focus on the resources inside of you and recognize what you are and aren't able to control. When we focus on what we can control, it increases our resilience, as well as making us feel happier, so when things don't work out we bounce back a lot quicker.

KEY POINTS TO REMEMBER

- It is important to work on building your success habits.
- Creating morning and evening routines will help you to thrive.
- Plan for energy and performance, and use this to inform how you spend your time.
- Take personal responsibility and accountability for what you do.
- Living by the 80/20 rule will help you to stay on track.

STEP THREE

Make a Plan to Take You Forward

You have looked at where you are and assessed where you want to go. Now it's about taking those steps to ensure that you make it happen. It's easy to imagine your future, but harder to be consistent in taking action to get there, especially when you add in "life" and what it may throw at you. In behavioural change terms, taking action is how those neural pathways become embedded and the brain's basal ganglia (see page 3) has assimilated the learning. This is the key to making stuff stick. You know where you are, have explored where you want to be and have made a plan. Now it is about being consistent (80 per cent of the time) in taking that action, despite whatever else is going on.

Although Rome wasn't built in a day, our culture focuses on quick results and when you don't achieve them as quickly as you perceive others to, it is easy to spiral into a comparison trap. This, in turn, erodes confidence and self-belief, leaving you stuck. I am sure I am not the only person who has bought into the "lose half a stone in a week" or "train for a 10k in 10 days" promises. As alluring as they sound, the results never match the bold claims and all you really lose is money and a bit of confidence, as you wonder if maybe you had done that bit more you would have got there.

This is a reminder that your journey toward change by using self-coaching will not be smooth and that part of this is about getting to know yourself and what is going on for you. Your self-awareness will increase which, in turn, will help you with your own relationships and make you happier. So, remember, even if it takes longer to achieve your goals, you will be getting lots of fringe benefits along the way.

The big questions that you will address in Step Three are:

- **How can I break down my goals into weekly actions?**
  You will be using a 90-day planning strategy, which
  includes a weekly review process to help keep you on track
  and accountable.
- **How can I accept all parts of myself?** You will be delving
  deeper into who you are, including looking at Jung's
  archetypes, building on the work from Step One.
- **How can I overcome obstacles?** You will be exploring
  how you can keep up your energy, and learning about
  the mindset and practical solutions you need to stay
  on track.

How to stick to your goals: grit and resilience

What makes some people stick to their goals, take action and get stuff done? We explored grittiness on page 139, and it is something that I witness in my work as well. You need a certain amount of grittiness and resilience, and you need to be able to market your skills alongside being able to deliver.

This ability to keep going and keep moving toward a set goal is something you can learn. It is part determination, part focus and part belief that you can get there, however long it takes. It is worth considering how much you truly believe that you can get to where you are going. If you don't believe right now, then part of what you need to do is build that belief. As James Clear says, "You need to believe before you be", meaning that the belief needs to come first to give you the push to act. This is why I recommend taking small consistent steps to help you build your belief. By doing so, you are more likely to think your big vision is achievable.

When I started my business, my first goal was to earn as much revenue as I did in my monthly salary. Now I know revenue doesn't equal income, but I was on a six-month notice period so figured if I knew I could get it in revenue, I could double it by the point when I would need to be paying myself. As I achieve each milestone, it helps build my belief that it is possible, especially as I have celebrated those milestones along the way!

Hand in hand with grit is resilience and the ability to bounce back when things don't work, because that can happen multiple times a day. As someone who runs two businesses, I have had multiple things not work out, including cash flow issues and staffing issues that have felt pretty grim. Each time something happens, I remind myself "this too will pass" and I take some time to reset and connect with a positive energy. This may well mean that I experience some negative emotions (and cry, often a lot) as I process what has happened, before I can pick myself up. The processing of these emotions needs to happen first, which is why self-awareness and self-care are often seen as critical parts of resilience. It is OK to take the space and time you need to process. Let your feelings, thoughts and bodily sensations be your compass, so that you know what you need to do before moving on.

You're in control of how you recover from setbacks. Yes, at first it hurts – it's not great when people say "no" or that project you thought was going to be a success flops. If you learn to see things as obstacles, rather than brick walls that you can't break down, it helps you to stay on track.

Remembering the big picture

What you will discover in this part of the book is designed to support you on your journey to change, helping you to integrate those new habits and ensuring that you stay on track with your vision. The work that you did in Step Two is relevant. The vision board you created and the visualization work is building those neural pathways, where you are seeing that change is possible. This is where you are headed, and it is always a great motivator to have this in mind when you are taking those smaller steps – everything adds up!

We are now moving from the imagination, the big picture, to integrating the plan and making it happen. The big picture is like an abstract painting – sometimes what we see in it changes and other times it feels clear.

Sometimes you need to remind yourself that just because you go off course at points it doesn't mean that your vision won't happen; you set your own timeline and you can adapt this if you need to. Often, it is motivating to know you have deadlines so you can measure your progress, as well as having that flexibility to change if needed.

In 2012, I was working at a school that was a three- to four-hour round commute. I visualized working somewhere closer to my house and how my life would change. I started applying for roles up to 30 minutes away and didn't get to the interview stage. There was a local secondary school, which I had a "feeling" I would work at one day. When the job came up, I imagined celebrating after receiving the phone call saying I was successful. It happened a few months later and my commute was slashed to a 10-minute walk!

Making it fun

One of the things which makes such a difference to how you feel is how you approach your future. Some people are obsessed with what might happen next and have a future focus. Although it is healthy to be optimistic, only focusing on what is going to happen next and living in the future can mean that you don't connect with where you are now.

I want to make the journey fun for you and am going to be talking about how you can enjoy where you currently are so that you are more likely to stick at it and start feeling better now, rather than only thinking of that as a future possibility.

Matching your identity and energy

I regularly support clients with acting as if something has already happened by using a future-focused visualization or even a simple question. Imagining that you have achieved your goal and you are already there, and connecting to that version of yourself energetically right now, can help you to change how you think, which in itself can have a transformative effect on how you feel. This works by building those neural pathways in the same way you do when you visualize. Connecting with the new identity you want to create, and stepping into it right now by considering what you want to let go of and what you want to do more of, can make you feel energized and confident.

Getting into the detail

The old adage is "if you fail to plan, you plan to fail". I would take this further in that if you fail to execute a plan, you will fail. Execution is what gets results, alongside integration. You need to be consistent with what you do to get the results that you want.

Let's consider the next 90 days. This planning timeline isn't unusual – it feels like a manageable "chunk" of time as it enables you to test and revise, gives you time to fall off the wagon and get back up, and it means that by the end you will be able to see the impact of your behavioural change. You're going to be breaking down your plan into weekly actions so you can stay on track and measure how you are getting on.

Identifying your blockers and barriers

Finally, you'll be looking at what is stopping you from exploring real and perceived barriers to your success and identifying what you can do to overcome them.

Sometimes, you may not be moving forward as you're cognitively overloaded, or maybe your nervous system is putting you into fight, flight, freeze or fawn mode (see page 3). You'll work through how you can stay in your window of tolerance, and move forward at your own pace with confidence and determination.

STEP THREE AIMS

- Be clear about your next steps.
- Commit to your actions.
- Get ready to step into joy and experience more positive emotions.
- Be positive about the journey ahead.
- Learn how to overcome obstacles.

7

Enjoying the Journey

We are now going to look at making the journey itself enjoyable and what can impede this happening. To experience the joy, you often need to lean into the not so nice emotions, as well and give yourself space to process and be honest about them.

In this chapter, you will explore:

- Self-acceptance at a deep and radical level
- Understanding your shadow side and accepting this as part of you
- Practising mindfulness and reducing your reliance on technology
- Stepping into the feelings of joy
- Changing your identity
- Embodying a frequency of love
- Ditching the fortune-telling

This is about giving you the toolkit to embody more joy on a daily basis and making the journey just as important as the destination.

So, how do we go from just a goal on a sheet of paper to making it happen? You may have written down that you want better relationships or a new job, or perhaps you are focused on making your health and wellbeing a priority. Whatever you want, this is your chance to make it happen.

It is time to break it down so that the goal becomes a plan, and you have actions and milestones that you can tick off. You can supercharge these by working on your energy and how you are showing up, as well as by starting to put in practices like visualization, which will help support what you are doing on a behavioural level. Keep in mind that behaviour doesn't change overnight – there isn't a switch you can flick to transform you into a different person.

Living in the here and now

As we discovered in the PERMA model (see page 95), one way of enhancing wellbeing and feeling better is by feeling more positive emotions. Part of the way that we can do this is to practice being more mindful and experience pleasure by living in the moment. There have been times in my life when I have been solely focused on the future and what I want to achieve, and it has left me not enjoying the moment. I learned that chasing goals without being in the present didn't make me happy so I transformed the way that I think about things, and now focus on living my life in the here and now, whilst working toward where I want to go. Not only do I feel calmer, I feel happier too.

This wasn't an overnight change; it was gradual. I realized I was no longer feeling "much" when I was achieving my goals and knowing the sacrifices that I had made to get there wasn't making me feel good. I relaxed and started to enjoy what was going on more. I became more curious and my success accelerated. That old adage that "slowing down to speed up" seems to be true, but why is this? When you slow down and give yourself space, you are often coming out of your sympathetic nervous system and reducing your stress levels. This is important as it means that more focus and energy can go to your prefrontal cortex, aiding decision-making and other areas of executive function. If you slow down, you are in a way supercharging your thinking and your cognitive abilities, so remember this when everything feels full on. Having time out can help you get more done (it can also greatly support your wellbeing and make you feel better).

Remember that when you are struggling to make decisions or solve problems, it is a sure sign that you may well be in a threat response and being flooded with stress hormones. Rather than pressurizing yourself to find the answer, take time out and reduce stress in whatever way you like to relax. When you have given yourself time and space, you are helping that journey toward your future goal as you are enhancing your cognition and thinking.

You are OK as you are

One of the things I have found makes a huge difference with my coaching clients and students is how they perceive themselves. I always say a red flag is when someone comes to you wanting to be fixed. I remember a client saying to me many years ago, "You are my last hope". I naively worked with them and quickly realized I had made a mistake. They expected me to have all the answers and do all the work for them – they were outsourcing their success.

You aren't broken, you don't need to be fixed. You are a glorious human right now and you are OK exactly as you are.

When you realize this and accept who you are, warts and all, things start to change; you are no longer preoccupied with the idea that life will start when you change an element of yourself. It starts now, today. You need to accept that you are OK right now and you are already loveable. To experience more joy in the journey, self-acceptance has to come first, which means liking all parts of you and all the things that you do.

In Step One, you did a whole heap of work on who you are and started to look at forgiveness and acceptance of yourself and we will be building on that here.

My turning point came around my weight. I have always been a normal weight, but two years of lockdown due to the pandemic, some family illness, perimenopause and the stress of moving house meant my weight shot up; not massively but enough to make me feel insecure. I was allowing it to impact me and was convinced that people would judge me on it. I had to do some pretty powerful self-coaching to realize this was about me: I was judging myself, no one else. I stopped making myself feel bad about my weight and accepted it. Of course, I then found losing the weight easier as it was no longer about needing to; it was more about wanting to.

The shadow and the light

Jung talked about the shadow and light that we all have. The shadow is made up of the characteristics that you aren't happy with or don't think are so desirable – for example, you may want to be direct and honest with people about what you think but bite your tongue so you don't upset them, or you might commit to doing things when you would prefer to be unsociable.

Jung's archetypes

A big part of Jung's work was to understand that the four archetypes, below, coexist in us and to appreciate all parts of us.

The Persona: This is how we present ourselves to the world and is the mask we wear in social situations. As children, we learn how we need to behave to fit in and we take our cues from others and the behaviours that we observe. Our persona allows us to adapt to the world around us and fit in with the society in which we live. The norms that we see are the ones we adapt to. If we become too closely identified with this archetype and this ability to fit in, we lose sight of ourselves as we can be chameleon-like in the way we are.

The Shadow: This exists in our unconscious mind and is made up of our repressed ideas, weaknesses, desires, instincts and perceived shortcomings. The shadow is formed as our persona develops, as we perceive things are undesirable through what we have observed and heard. This is often seen as our dark side. Often, people may deny this element of themselves and instead project onto others – for example, if they feel they are selfish, they may call others selfish.

The Anima or Animas: This is the feminine image in the male psyche/the male image in the female psyche. It represents the true self.

The Self: This is a combination of our unconscious and conscious parts, with the ego at the centre. This is who we truly are and how we operate.

If you are avoiding the parts of you that you feel are undesirable, you may well be stopping yourself from truly growing. Unless you do this work around self-acceptance, you will struggle to live in joy and this is really what this is about – letting go of some of the things that are preventing that.

Consider how often you are not operating from the space of who you really are and adapting to what you believe is expected of you. Often, I see people who have worked in a specific role for a long time and have adapted and moulded themselves to be a certain way. If this resonates, remember you can get to know yourself again by looking at things like your values (see page 72).

A great perspective is that we all have parts of ourselves that, for whatever reason, we keep hidden or we don't like as much as other parts. When we are accepting of all our parts, we feel happier and more content. This is a reminder that perfection doesn't exist and that when we practise genuine self-acceptance we are OK with every element of ourselves. This is important to highlight now as if you start from this basis and build upwards, you are likely to be much more accepting and connected to your journey.

Identifying your shadow side

It can be hard to access our unconscious; answering the questions below may give you some insight. Remember to practise self-care when you are doing any work like this. If you feel emotional, take a step back and ask for support.

1) When do you feel triggered or activated by someone or something?

2) What do you dislike the most about yourself?

3) What do you dislike in others?

4) Who, if anyone, do you hold a grudge against? What keeps you stuck in the grudge?

5) What personality traits from your family/parents/caregivers do you dislike? How many of these do you see in yourself?

6) If you are a parent, what personality traits do you dislike in your children? How many of these do you see in yourself?

7) What elements of your personality would you like to change?

8) When have you been criticized personally? What did people say?

9) How frequently do you feel you need to wear a mask with others? What do you dial down/up about yourself?

10) What are your biggest fears?

Reliance on technology

There is nothing worse than being with someone one-to-one and them being on their phone. So, why do we do it? It is because we get a dopamine hit as our brain associates being on our phone/social media with pleasure, so we start to anticipate that we will be experiencing pleasure and pick up our phones without really knowing why, then end up looking at our screens rather than the people around us. I spoke about creating "friction" earlier on in the book (see page 100) and if you want more joy, it is time to break up with your phone or at least have a less intense relationship with it. Although you see pleasure as a by-product of being on your devices, over time, this feeling will erode.

It's time to step into the joy

Joy is one of the raft of positive emotions which make up positive affect in the PERMA model (see page 95). The more you experience it, the more you improve your wellbeing. When you experience joy, there is more activity in the prefrontal cortex area of the brain and that all-important dopamine is released. Reinforcing the relationship between an experience and that feeling of pleasure strengthens your neural pathways and means your brain will have a preference to seek out the experience or behaviour.

By tapping into joy and other positive emotions you will experience a whole raft of benefits:

- Decreased levels of stress, which can improve your cognitive abilities and your wellbeing.
- An increase in your ability to think creatively and notice opportunities.
- Improved wellbeing, as discussed in the PERMA model.
- A movement toward reward, which helps open up our thinking and energy in the prefrontal cortex – the area of the brain focused on decision-making, memory and problem-solving

I have worked with many clients who believe that when they are thinner/richer/fill in the blank, they will do X and Y. When you get to that milestone, nothing is going to be different – although you really will be older! This deferral of pleasure and inability to live in the moment can make you feel disengaged and demotivated and, although you may reach your destination, it isn't going to make you feel good.

Your daily diet of joy is critical to feeling better and life is too short not to prioritize it. If you are stuck or feeling overwhelmed, I can guarantee that by focusing on joy you are going to be rewiring your brain's neural pathways and opening up your thinking to more creativity. Imagine you are building your emotional "muscle memory" whilst you are doing this.

Your box of joy

Ask yourself honestly when you last experienced joy or pleasure or awe. Start to think about how you can increase your daily quota of positive emotions, whilst focusing on your goal. Imagine you have a box of joy that contains the things that give you that feeling. That make you smile and twinkle just by looking at them.

What is in your box? Now, consider how can you get your dose in.

In my joy box are my cuddles with my husband, sitting with a coffee looking at my garden, a walk in the forest, my kids, my friends, a perfect avocado, that feeling when you have finished a run (yes, I am one of those people who enjoys running). The list goes on.

Flexible goals

Keep in mind that your goal may change as you move toward it and that it may be impacted by what else is going on. The steps that you take to achieve your goal and work toward success need to be flexible due to external events, such as a restructuring in the company you work at or a global recession. Personal matters, such as a family member getting ill, may also alter what is important to you right now.

In all these instances you can only control how you respond and what you do next. Sometimes, things don't work out and the most important thing is to reflect on what you have learned from the experience and what you will do differently in the future, rather than dwelling on what could have been.

This links into the idea of growth mindset. When you believe that you are capable of improving and learning from what you have been doing, then you are much more likely to keep going. When you believe that your abilities are fixed, you are much more likely to give up.

This is the time to truly embody a growth mindset and appreciate that success is not linear, and that roadblocks are there to test you. I always like to reflect on some of the lessons that I receive from "the universe" by considering what these things mean and what they are telling me e.g, when I got up early one morning to go to the gym and it was closed, what was the lesson? I realised it was a sign that I needed to be more prepared and organized, and saw it as an opportunity to focus on planning ahead.

One of my clients was going through a rather messy divorce and was concerned that she was going to lose her family home. We worked together to look at what she could and couldn't control. She could control paying her mortgage, speaking to solicitors and how she communicated with her soon to be ex-husband. She couldn't control if he contributed financially, or what he did or said to her or the children. When she was able to make a plan based on her behaviour, it decreased the overwhelm and, although the situation was not very pleasant, she felt like she was handling it in a more confident way.

You can see lessons everywhere. They may not be lessons from the universe if you don't believe in a higher being or bigger influence, but they're still lessons and when you are open to seeing the learning or the humour in a situation it is much easier to steer forward and continue to progress.

Identity change and becoming who you want to be

You may be faltering with moving toward your goal if your identity doesn't match your future vision. You need to be able to step into that vision and the identity of the person that you want to become. Identity change is critical, and it starts with the belief that you can become the person that you want to be and the person who has achieved these goals.

This is why it's important to vibrate in a "frequency of love", which is the highest frequency you can be in. So, what does this mean? David Hawkins, spiritual teacher and author, developed the map of consciousness over a 20-year period, where he conducted more than 250,000 calibrations defining a range of values, attitudes and emotions. Calibrations measure the frequency of movement, effectively saying that for each emotion there is a different frequency. This scale, which goes from 1 to 1,000, is often referred to as levels of consciousness, measuring our state and emotion and its frequency. When you're vibrating at your lowest frequencies, such as guilt and shame, you tend not to be energetically attractive to others or only attract those at a similar frequency. Imagine a time when you have been feeling ashamed of something you have done and then going with that feeling into a job interview or a first date; you are not going to be bringing your best self.

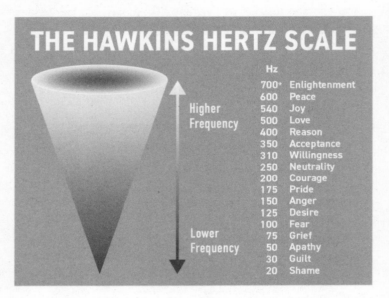

THE HAWKINS HERTZ SCALE

Hz	
700+	Enlightenment
600	Peace
540	Joy
500	Love
400	Reason
350	Acceptance
310	Willingness
250	Neutrality
200	Courage
175	Pride
150	Anger
125	Desire
100	Fear
75	Grief
50	Apathy
30	Guilt
20	Shame

Higher Frequency

Lower Frequency

If you're looking at this from an energetic point of view, it is about vibrating at the frequency that you want to become, so really embodying what success looks and feels like and how this shows up in your life. You can get a sense of what frequency you're vibrating at by reflecting on the emotions that you're feeling. You don't click your fingers and achieve your goal. Instead, consider who you need to be to achieve your goal and how you need to be.

I remember when I made the commitment to find a partner. I was fed up with being single so I was proactive and, as a result, I met new people, which was a big achievement for me. I also acted as if I was in a relationship with myself. I worked on my confidence and my communication skills, as well as how I wanted to be when I met someone, which was calm and relaxed. In a few months, I had met the man who is now my husband, although there were a few frog kisses along the way!

The point is you need to be the match for your desires energetically. It's the age-old adage "dress for the job you want, not the job you have". Show up for the person you will be when you have achieved your goal, not the person you are now. Consider what you need to do more of and what you need to do less of. This will help you to energetically attract more of what you want and less of what you don't want, and can only support you on your journey toward your goal.

When you are feeling in a higher vibration and experiencing positive emotion, such as love or joy, you become more attractive to others. We know confidence is attractive, so is our state. As someone with a background in sales, we were told to "face the dial with a smile" – the reason being that when we have positive emotions, we are more attractive to speak to. Consider how you can reframe how you are feeling and how you are able to get into a frequency of love.

Part of this is about being aware of what you're feeling and how you can reframe emotions when you need to. This isn't about toxic positivity, where you pretend that everything is fine when really it isn't, or about discrediting negative emotions – they are there for a reason and I believe feeling them, acknowledging them and understanding their source helps you to increase your self-awareness and emotional intelligence. In fact, this is about working through the emotions and then changing your state as you actively choose to feel differently. It may be easier to do this in some situations than others.

Positive attracts positive and negative attracts negative is a good rule of thumb for life. Again, this doesn't mean you need to be relentlessly positive. At times you do need to create space to be sad, angry, upset, resentful etc.

Tuning in

When you are feeling a negative emotion, what is going on?
- How and where do you feel it in your body?
- What are you thinking?
- What are your bodily sensations and thoughts telling you?
- What do you want to do as a result?
- How do you want to feel as an alternative?
- What can you do to tap into that positive emotion and feeling?

What you're doing here is identifying and acting in a way that is consistent with how you want to feel and show up.

Fortune-telling

How often do you go into a situation and think you already know what is going to happen – perhaps something that is high stakes, such as a job interview or a first date? You decide in your mind what will happen and then project that onto the situation and, guess what, it ends up happening. You then tell yourself, "I told you so …". Now, imagine you change that crystal ball into a positive end game. How does it change how you show up? How is what you do different?

Remember, you cannot predict the future so, instead, take a step back and look at what you can control. Focus on those outcomes. By being more intentional with your desires and what you are telling yourself, you can start to positively imagine outcomes rather than being stuck in negative thinking styles.

The message from this chapter is loud and clear – make the process fun and connect in with yourself now. You are on a journey toward your ideal future, and you don't know how long that journey will take. Enjoying it on the way will make a big difference.

KEY POINTS TO REMEMBER

- Stay open-minded to change.
- Become aware of your shadow side and work on your self-acceptance.
- There is real power in staying present.
- Keep tapping into your joy as you progress on your journey.
- Embody who you want to become.

8

Making Change Happen

Now it's time to drill down from that big goal into your 90-day plan. This is the blueprint that will help determine what you do on a day-to-day basis, and will bring in some strategic thinking to help you approach your goal in a more concrete, less abstract way. In terms of those neural pathways, consider these action steps as ways to reinforce the visualization and future-focus work you have been doing. This is where you are going to see those compound effects.

In this chapter, you will explore how to:

- Clarify your big goal and focus
- Break down the goal into actionable steps
- Map out the time and resources you need for your goals
- Focus on fun when building your dreams

What is your big goal?

Connect back to your big goal from Step Two. When you write it down, check it is still what you want to achieve and notice how it feels in your body, and energetically, as well as how it makes you think. Remember that our energy around things is linked to our emotion: if you are not feeling excited, it is worth reflecting on why that is. When I work with coaching clients, I always talk about congruence and this means:

- Does how you feel match what you are thinking?
- Does everything feel aligned – for example, do your bodily sensations match your emotion and your thoughts?
- How much do you want this?

You want to be in a place where your mind, emotions and body are all feeling the same thing and, if you are thinking about your goal, it is about excitement and motivation. If you don't feel motivated, then it is worth revisiting your goal. Although grittiness and stickability are useful to achieve our goals, they need to be aligned with our values and motivation. "How much does this goal still mean to me?" is a great reflective question. If the goalposts have moved and you ignore those feelings, you are never going to achieve what you desire. In my experience, it is the meaningful goals that work better.

One of the terms I coined early on in my business is "me too" goals. Someone might say they want to earn £5,000 a month or only work 20 hours a week, and then a whole host of others would say me too. And here is the thing ... you often believe the me-too goal because of social desirability and wanting to fit in. If everyone wants a Range Rover Vogue and you don't, does that mean you are different? The answer is yes. What is important is embracing this difference and doing the things which matter to you, rather than those which matter to others. There is no point building someone else's life or creating a life which looks brilliant on social media, but in reality feels "meh". Your life, your rules and your goals – be sure that these are the right ones!

Walking your timeline

This is an NLP (Neuro-Linguistic Programming) exercise, all about having a physical connection with the steps and actions you need to take, which I have adapted. I find it effective as the combination of physically moving and thinking helps me think clearly and connect with what I want. You will need a partner to help you.

1. Stand on the floor and ensure you have at least 20m (65ft) in front of you. If you don't have this space inside, go outside into a wide-open space.

2. Stand on a spot that represents today's date and time and look into the future. Walk to a future spot 90 days in the future and stop. Tell your partner what date this spot represents and what you have achieved (your goal), then take a step backwards. Tell your partner what date this represents and what you are doing to help you achieve the goal. Then, take steps back until you reach the current date. When you are there, walk forward through each step. As you are doing this, notice if the order of the steps feels right and if there is anything that you would take out or add in.

3. Now write all this down. As you are writing, if you feel that any of the steps are dependent on something else happening, write that in e.g., if you are talking about starting a new role, consider what you need in order to apply and how you will find the role. If you can create a sequence of steps, you are starting to create your plan.

Your 90-day plan

The timeline you have worked out forms the basis of the plan, which you can start to populate further. Begin by honing in on the next 90 days:

- What is the one thing you want to achieve over these 90 days?
- What are the things you need to have in place to achieve this?
- How do you need to be to achieve this? Consider what you need to be thinking, what you need to be feeling and the way that you need to show up to achieve this goal.
- What support do you need?

Before you start with the weekly plan (overleaf), ask yourself the questions below to solidify your thinking, leading on from what you have just done and using the structure we have already spoken about.

1) What is my goal for the next 90 days? Make it a SMART goal: Specific, Measurable, Achievable, Realistic and Time Bound (see page 120).
2) What do I need to believe about myself to make this happen?
3) How will I feel when I have achieved this? This is a great point to do a future visualization (see page 112) and imagine you have achieved this 90-day goal to tap into your emotions and how you are feeling and thinking. The visualization might also help you with steps, and can build on what you did with the NLP exercise opposite.

4) What support and resources do I need? Consider who you have around you and where you need to ask for help in making this happen.

I hope you are feeling excited and ready to go with your plan!

Weekly planning meeting

At the start of each week, I recommend you have a meeting with yourself. I do this on a Sunday night as it helps to set me up for the week and to feel motivated and energized. If you are more of a morning person, you might prefer to do it on Monday morning. You might want to ask yourself:

1) What are my goals this week?
2) What do I need to believe about myself and my abilities to make this happen?
3) What success measures will I use? (i.e., how will I know I have achieved the goals?)
4) How do these achievements link into my 90-day goal?
5) How will I celebrate on Friday?
6) What support and resources do I need?

Example answers:

1) To journal three times this week, to read at least one chapter of a self-development book (maybe this one!), to exercise three times for at least 30 minutes.
2) I need to believe that I can stick to the plan and have the motivation to do so.

3) I want to be clearer on my next steps career-wise, so journalling will help me. I want to understand my strengths more so the book will help. I want to feel healthier so will use exercise to do this.
4) I need to believe I can change my career and that I can find the answers.
5) I will meet up with a friend without my phone.
6) I need to make sure that I get enough sleep and that I finish work when I am meant to. I need to block out my lunch hours for exercise.

Make sure you have time scheduled into your diary to take action, whether it is going for a walk for 30 minutes three times a week, studying a topic you want to learn more about, planning your meals or having time with your partner. The most important thing is that you set the goals and actions and you execute against them. Scheduling the time into your calendar is one of the easiest ways I have found to stick to a plan.

I often over-commit and for years my diary looked like a mess. Luckily, I now have an excellent PA who works for me part-time. She blocks out lunch and gym sessions each week so I can't put anything else in. Because my calendar is linked up to everything else, it means no one can book in time with me either. Using electronic calendars makes things easier as I can set up alerts and colour code things to clearly see how much time I am spending on my goals.

When you have the weekly planning meeting with yourself, I recommend that you do a mini visualization. As you know, this helps build your neural pathways. I like this method as it blends being strategic with science.

Tracking your progress: weekly CEO meeting

When you set goals, it is essential to follow up on your progress. Schedule some time each week, perhaps on a Friday, so you can review what you have done that week.

These questions can guide the meeting:

- What was my goal at the beginning of the week?
- How did I get on?
- What did I do well?
- Where do I need to focus next week?
- What have I learned about myself?
- What have I learned about the situation?
- How will this learning impact what I do next?

The answers to these questions then inform the goal-setting/planning process for the following week. The tracking session creates a continuous feedback loop for yourself. I liken it to being at Weight Watchers, where you have a weekly weigh in – this is your weekly goal check-in. Remember to celebrate your progress and learning too: it is vital for building those new neural pathways.

Combining the logical and intuitive

The logical, the emotive and the intuitive often go together. You make a logical plan, which has dates and activities, and then you have the structure. You commit to daily (or weekly) action and then each week you reflect on where you are and what you have achieved, as well as how you feel emotionally and intuitively.

Our brains are wired with a preference basis and you can, through neuroplasticity, develop different thinking styles and ways of looking at things. When you exercise cognitive agility, you allow yourself to see things more holistically and you have congruence between what you are thinking, feeling and doing. This is where you often feel that sensation of alignment and calmness as you navigate what is next.

This is worth building into your planning as you can be guided by data and evidence, alongside how you feel about something. The CEO meetings are important as you look at what has happened and then reflect on how you are feeling: this is data and if you are not on the right path, it can bring that into your awareness. It is common to persist with goals, despite evidence that suggests you need to stop. This is down to the economic theory of "sunk costs" – if you have spent a lot of money investing in training and then realize you don't enjoy what you are learning, you might persist with it due to the money spent. An alternative way of looking at this is to understand that the training itself offered a good investment because you now know it isn't for you. You learnt something about yourself from it.

Checking in with how things feel to you and what your intuition and energy are telling you can be useful when you are working toward new goals, and remember there are no dead ends, only learning! If you find that you aren't where you want to be in your CEO meetings, or you are not feeling motivated or energized, this is learning so recognize this and celebrate it too!

Planning the time for your goals

I hear a lot of people saying "I don't have time" to pursue my goal or get things done. Now, as far as we do all have the same 24 hours in the day (thanks Kim K), we all also have different constraints on our time. I think, like most things, we have the reality and the perceived reality.

If you are a single mum of three kids, one with additional needs, and you are working part-time you will have less time than a single person working full-time. This is the reality. Everyone has commitments, and some of us have more commitments than others. It doesn't help to compare your time frames with others, so focus on you and what you can do rather than looking externally.

I am going to help you get clear on where you spend your time so you can start to think about the choices that you have. I like to split it into non-negotiable commitments such as your work, caring responsibilities and sleep, and then the areas of life where you have more control over what you do. The following activities will help you to get clarity on where you can gain some more time, even if it is minimal.

Do, Ditch, Delegate, Automate

This is a great activity to help you get clarity on what you have going on and what you could potentially get rid of or delegate.

1) Write down everything that you do on a weekly basis. This can include your work, if you want to, or it can just include home life, hobbies etc. If you are struggling to write this from scratch, write things down as they happen each week and then look at this at the end of the week in your CEO meeting. This is one of those activities that you can keep coming back to as more things come to mind.

2) Look at the list you have written and separate it out under Do, Ditch, Delegate and Automate headings:

a) What do only you need to do? This stays on the Do list.

b) What do you want to do that will help you get closer to your goals as well as feeling better and happier? You can add things which you may not be currently doing here?

c) What could you ditch altogether and it would have no impact on your ability to achieve your goals or enhance your life? Write that down here e.g., it may be that you are going to ditch your daily Instagram scroll or watching Netflix every night. You get to choose. When you are looking at what you will ditch, consider what you will gain in terms of time.

d) What could you delegate? Traditionally, we think about delegation models from work, where we get other team members to take on elements of our roles. You can also think about delegation in terms of your home life, both within your family or housemates, where you live and amongst friends. If you are the one who always organizes get-togethers, how about asking friends if they would take it in turns?

e) And the final one, which is one of my favourites, what can you automate? E.g., you may have a supermarket delivery on repeat each week or pay bills by direct debit. Think creatively about whether there is anything you do now which could be automated.

Now look at the list. Where have you gained time? How much time do you now have to focus on your goals?

People often split their 24-hour day into eight hours of sleep, eight hours of work and eight hours of leisure, but this doesn't account for the time it takes to get ready for bed and showering etc, so really it is probably closer to 10 hours for sleep and self-care. Work may not just be what you do for a living. There is unpaid work in the home, as well as paid work. This is about being brutally honest with yourself about what your capacity is, and then seeing how this links to your plan. Remember, it is a marathon not a sprint so if you have limited time and it takes longer to reach your goal, then it takes longer!

Finally, we don't need to fill up every scrap of space in our diary to be "productive". In fact, for most of us being faced with a diary which is jam-packed will be overwhelming and, as a result, we are likely to retreat and do nothing. So, instead, create some white space and flex so that you don't set yourself an impossible task.

Even if you can dedicate ten minutes a day to achieving your new goal, you will start to form new habits and habitual behaviours, which will help you to move forward. The trick here is to make this as bite-sized as possible to increase your chances of succeeding, rather than floundering at the first step and feeling like you are failing.

My basic life hack when I started my business was to stop watching TV, which used to be my pastime for three or four evenings a week. Instead, I started to devote time to my personal development, as well as starting my business on social media. I still don't really watch TV. I watch movies and am much more likely to read a book or chat to friends. This is what works for me. What works for you may be very different. Consider where you have flex and what you can let go of.

I'm now aware of the things that I have sacrificed along the way. Now that I know the importance of connecting to the joy of the journey, I wouldn't do it again. I would go back and spend the time with loved ones, dance at parties and travel to see people. I listened to a podcast years ago about sacrifice and took it far too literally. Now, my ethos is around feeling good, being happy and achieving my goals in a way that works for me. If it takes me a bit longer as I am so busy living and loving, then I believe I am on the right path.

When we moved into our dream house, we had visitors every weekend for months: the house itself has such a great energy and it is perfect for entertaining. I realized that it represented what was so important in my life and had been lacking at times, especially during the pandemic. This was part of my happiness project and something that I didn't even realize was so important to me. Hosting my daughter's party and finishing up at 2am sitting round the fire chatting with good friends gave me warm fuzzy feelings, and created memories I will never forget.

You may want to revisit your list regularly to check in with what fun activities you have ditched, and to consider how you can have fun whilst still pursuing your goals and changing your life. Remember that relationship between pleasure and building new neural pathways has a heap of evidence behind it, so embrace it!

KEY POINTS TO REMEMBER

- Break down your goal into actionable steps.
- Plan for success with milestones and targets.
- Consider when you can work on your goals.
- Identify how you can gain back some time.
- Focus on the fun whilst you are building your dreams.

9

Overcoming Obstacles

You picked up this book as you had great intentions to change an element, or elements, of your life and live in a way that was more aligned and in tune with what you wanted. However, life often gets in the way. It is OK to have fallen out of the saddle or not even started yet. In this chapter, you are going to explore what could be going on and how you can move forward with purpose.

When you look at blocks and barriers, your brain can immediately go to what you can't do, as it searches for perceived threats. Remember, this process then takes away energy from the prefrontal cortex and the areas of the brain responsible for deeper thinking, processing and learning. It is why I will be talking about how you can approach obstacles using more positive language. So, rather than asking the classic coaching question "What is stopping you?", which can put you into that threat response where you start to search for what could be wrong, I will be asking, "What do you need to succeed?" By focusing on moving toward a future goal, you are working with the brain's pleasure centre and that all-important dopamine.

In this chapter, you will explore:

- The resources that you need to be successful
- How to build that all important self-belief
- Your window of tolerance and comfort zone
- The games you may be playing unconsciously and how to step out of these

What resources do you need?

Why do some people achieve and others don't? We all know of someone who appears to be lucky and always gets what they want. The key is they believe in themselves and what they are doing. If you energetically believe in yourself, you are much more likely to take inspired, aligned action than if you don't. Plus, we know people can feel our energy: if it has a high vibe, it is attractive.

Now, bring to mind that person you are going to become. Tap back into that imagery you created in the last part of the book. What resources do you need to achieve this? Maybe it is about asking for help, having some proactive conversations or merely giving yourself permission to get over yourself and start taking action.

Resources may include practical things. For example, to write this book, I needed a laptop and a printer so that I could read and work on the drafts, which I did on lots of coffee! If you want to build your fitness, you might need trainers, weights or a gym membership. If you are working at home, part of your resource might be creating an area in your house which you can dedicate to work. This was one of the biggest gamechangers for me. Around three years into my business, I decided to take it more seriously and converted our lounge into my office. I got a desk, chair and some nice plants and pictures. We still had the sofa in there and chilled out in it at times, but it was mainly my space. The resource of space and the physical objects made me change how I viewed my business, and it has grown since then. Now, I have my own office in the house, as well as a garden office.

Resources can equally include people who may support you – if you look back to the Do, Ditch, Delegate, Automate exercise (see page 184), these may be people who you can delegate some of your tasks to at work, or maybe your partner or a family member who can support you outside of work. As well as helping you to achieve your goals, resources are the things that will give you more time to focus on your goals.

Part way through writing this book, I was going through a period of feeling stuck in my business. Our growth had stagnated and I started to fixate on what I didn't like. I found the more I focused on what I didn't like, the more it was there. My energetic vibration was probably scraping along the floor and it felt heavy. Working with my energy coach, I reflected on what I loved about my business – the freedom it gave me, the impact I had, and I realized that I do love my business. I switched up my energy and there was a massive shift.

At a similar time, we got a new trainer into the business, who had a deep understanding of neuroscience. He was challenging me about some of the content (which is what I wanted) and it made me think more deeply about how to train our coaches more effectively and how to frame things in this book. One thing that emerged was that we were often asking questions that we thought would be helpful, but that could throw our clients into overwhelm. This can happen when you are self-coaching as well.

Your energetic resources

Your state and energy impact everything. When you're dragging yourself along, you're hardly inspirational or a joy to be around. That is why it is so useful to track your energy and to be selfish when you feel you need time to recharge. It is something I have become famous for amongst my friends – I have modelled to them that it is OK to meet your needs first.

How do you switch up your energy? When I work with clients and they are feeling "flat" or low on energy, some of the things I recommend they try are:

- Somatic shaking – when you stand and shake every part of your body
- Stretching
- Star jumps
- Walking barefoot outdoors and grounding into the floor
- Asking questions to help them tap into gratitude or positive affect
- Dancing

My clients choose what they want to try, and I encourage you to do the same. Play around with the different ideas and notice which ones help you shift your energy and change your mood.

Tuning into your needs is such an important process and it is one that I encourage you to keep practising. In fact, it works with most things – working from home, the distance from me to the kitchen is about 30 steps. I stand there opening drawers and cupboards (considering we are people who don't cook, we have a lot of these). I do it automatically, and then usually end up with a piece of fruit, which is kept on the side so you can see it, therefore the friction between seeing it and eating it is limited. When I do open a cupboard and find some chocolate or crisps, I ask myself, "What do I need?". Often, I need to sit with my feelings, or go outside or get off my laptop.

REFLECTION

Start practising these questions when you feel that you are drained energetically or that something is off:
- What is this feeling telling me?
- What do I need?

The power of self-belief

We looked at self-belief in Step Two and I am returning to it now as I can hypothesize that sometimes the wall that you are failing to scale is due to your lack of self-belief. When you are able to overcome these barriers, you may find a door that you can pass through instead.

The good news is that self-belief is a muscle: one that you can build, like we build and grow any of our other muscles. I shared the scaling exercise (see page 89) that worked for me earlier. Another way you can work on self-belief is by considering who you will model. Psychologist Albert Bandura developed social learning theory in the 1970s. In his work, he looked at how children learn and noted that observing what others do is critical. When I coach leaders, we work on modelling behaviours – for example, "leaving loudly" describes when you leave the office to go to the gym, see your parents or pick up your kids (or anything else). It is a great technique to let teams know it is OK to work flexibly.

REFLECTION

When you are considering modelling behaviours, think of someone you know, who appears to display high levels of self-belief. Reflect on these questions:

- What behaviours does the person exhibit that show self-belief?
- How do they communicate with others?
- What do you think they believe about themselves?

The person may be someone you work with or a friend, or it could be someone who is really good at something you want to achieve. E.g., if you want to become a good tennis player, you might study Serena Williams and how she shows up on court. It is less about observing her tennis skills and more about how she holds herself, and the way she moves and behaves on the court.

When you have completed your study of the person you have chosen, reflect on what will you do differently as a result. Start to model these behaviours when you can – remember, like everything, you start small and then adapt, depending on how it feels and the feedback you receive from others.

Mindset

The way you think about yourself and your ability will impact how likely you are to keep going. Your resilience and grit impact how you stick to your goals and the plan and, when the going gets tough, whether the tough get going or stay going.

Hal Elrod, author and motivational speaker, refers to people who are "miracle mavens" and achieve the things that others don't. The ingredients of being a maven includes an unshakable self-belief (and putting in significant effort).

So, how do you build self-belief? The answer is by practising. Start to notice when you stop yourself from doing things because you are not ready/you don't feel good enough/you are too old/too young. This limiting behaviour is what is keeping you stuck.

Having a good growth mindset is essential. The first attempt at doing anything new will need refinement. It is normal to fall down or make a mistake. If you can take the learning from this and use it in a forward motion, rather than berating yourself, things change. Remember, you can make a conscious choice to believe your results aren't dependent on your ability and being committed to improvement and development.

I know which one I choose and, of course, at times I don't. I slip back into those patterns – convincing myself I am too old, not smart enough etc. These are the times when I bring my self-coach to the fore and ask "What can I do right now?" And, guess what, there is always an answer, always something more I can do. The only person who is able to flip this switch in your head is you. The question is how are you ensuring that you do?

What are you saying to yourself?

Our diet is key to self-belief. I am not talking kale and broccoli, although these will help your brain. I am talking about the language that we feed our brains. It is so easy to get into those circles of self-criticism, when all you focus on is what you have done wrong.

These could be small things: maybe you decide not to have that conversation with someone at work, as deep down you don't feel confident enough in what you do and who you are.

That may limit you achieving your goal of a promotion as you fail to network and build relationships.

Your beliefs won't be changed overnight. In Step Two, we looked at how beliefs are linked to identity change and how you build neural pathways to support the beliefs over time. As you strengthen a pathway, it may become the "go-to" belief but your old pathway will still be there and may be reignited if you are triggered by something which takes you back to those old patterns.

Instead of focusing on limiting language, consider what beliefs would enhance your ability to achieve your goals and would give you the confidence to go for it.

Reflective practice

Reflective practice is designed to help you look for solutions by focusing on the positive – you are opening up your thinking to consider the possibilities. From this positive frame, you can start to ask yourself how you could change your behaviour and what you can learn from where you are. This can help to give you clarity and unscramble the spaghetti in your head, so that you are able to move forward and start to understand your patterns. Think about your frame of reference as constructive and future-focused, which is one of the premises of coaching.

REFLECTION

Journal, reflecting on the following questions:
- What am I saying to myself that is unhelpful?
- What beliefs would help me right now?

- What can I say to myself that is helpful?
- What do I need to hear right now?
- How can I make the most of this situation?

Doing the work

I tell my clients that the work is like peeling an onion. Each time you take off one layer there is another one underneath, although you might never get to the core. Keeping the onion analogy going, the work may well make you cry at times and bring out emotional responses – this is normal. When people talk about "doing the work", it is about confronting your truths and often having those uncomfortable conversations with yourself about what you have done to get into your current situation. We are all culpable, although we have to remember it is evolution and nature that are often keeping us safe.

Your nervous system and window of tolerance

If you push too far out of your comfort zone, it isn't only your brain that senses a threat – your sympathetic nervous system will be activated, which can take you into fight or flight mode, causing anxiety, panic or freeze, where you become numb and unable to act. Focusing on the threat means the battery power needed to run all your executive functions in your prefrontal cortex is diminished. The result is you can no longer think as effectively, your working memory is impacted and you struggle to problem-solve. If you need any other reminder not to push too far out of your comfort zone, this is it!

The balance is in keeping you safe, feeling calm and connected to yourself, so you are gradually moving out of your comfort zone but not too far into your stretch zone. We know the magic happens outside our comfort zone; we all have a window of tolerance within which we can operate most effectively. It is where you can function well cognitively and effectively process stimuli. Your executive functions such as decision-making, problem-solving and thinking are working well, and you can perform effectively. This is where you ideally need to be when you are working on your goals.

Your window of tolerance is affected by your emotions – the safer and more supported you are, the more you can stay within your window. So, consider the support that you have around you. If you feel that you don't have enough, how can you get more? It might be that you ask your boss for help or you lean more on friends. Equally, if you are struggling in this area, you might want to look at something around support in your 90-day plan, such as finding a mentor at work, getting a coach or building new relationships and friendships.

Avoidance

We all have negative patterns of behaviour and can self-sabotage at times. In fact, ask any author (me included) what they have done instead of writing and you will probably get a list as long as your arm, including everything from having a super-tidy house to a phone addiction. The reasons we don't write? We probably don't truly feel energized in that moment. If we can take a step back and do something to change our state, we can be more engaged with what we have to do.

Who are you being? Child vs Parent

The work of psychiatrist Eric Berne, the founder of Transactional Analysis (TA), puts an interesting spin on the roles that we play, which may self-sabotage. This is relevant here as it is about starting to notice patterns of behaviour in how we communicate with others.

There are five ego states that he says we can go into:

- Adapted child
- Free child
- Critical parent
- Nurturing parent
- Adult

The healthiest state to be in is adult but we may find that we slip into other states, which impacts our communication and connection.

For example, a critical parent may always want to be in charge and decide what "should" happen. They are often critical of others and their choices.

The nurturing parent, by contrast, looks after people – they are always that shoulder to cry on and they often put others' needs above their own.

As children, we observe these parental behaviours and take them on as our own. As an adult, you can be triggered back into these states and act from the part you have adopted – for example, if your partner isn't behaving in the way you want, you may find yourself adopting a critical parent role, telling them what they have done is wrong, or a nurturing role where you are much more supportive of them and making sure they are OK.

If you are in "parent" mode, you won't be treating them like an adult. Instead, you will be seeing them as a child. Recognizing that you have stepped into one of these behaviours can be the first step to changing them.

Reflect on when you have found yourself taking on either a critical or nurturing parent role. I find that I am the nurturing parent with my children and family but I can go into critical parent at work, especially when I am stressed. I remember speaking to a team member who had made the same mistake multiple times. She was heavily in child mode and I realized I had stepped into parent mode when she said, "I feel like I am being told off". I reflected that my behaviour needed some work as it wasn't an adult-to-adult conversation.

We may find ourselves taking on the "child" role, replaying our behaviours and thinking from childhood. We may be a free or rebellious child, who doesn't like rules or restrictions. I have even seen myself get into this role with my children! Or we might be more obedient and follow instructions, whilst looking for guidance from a parent.

Finally, there are adult states, which is where you respond to the here and now rather than from one of the internalized parent or child states. In "adult", you can have much more effective conversations with others: they are your equal, rather than being above or below you. This makes for much healthier and effective communication.

You will find you often play out different roles, depending on your environment and context.

Drivers and games that we all play

In addition to the child/parent model, Eric Berne proposed that we all have preferred drivers which impact how we show up and may be the reason why we revert to an old identity or behaviour. These drivers can map onto some of the personality preferences that you found out about in Step One (see page 49). Remember that they are the things that have been with you from childhood, and you will have developed them as coping mechanisms.

These are the common drivers from Transactional Analysis (TA):

1. **Hurry up:** The "hurry up" driver does what it says on the tin and gets you to do things at a fast pace. If you have this preference, you may be getting a lot done but not feeling present in what you do.

2. **Be strong:** This driver believes that showing emotions isn't good and you need to be "tough". You may find it hard to connect with your feelings, which can result in illness or depression.

3. **Try hard:** This driver has a go at things, but can get bored and give up. They tend to have lots of things on the go, struggle with endings and feel like a failure.

4. **Please others**: This driver works hard to keep others happy and puts them before themselves. They may have a wide circle of friends, but often don't get their own needs met and may feel resentful of this.

5. **Be perfect:** This driver likes everything to be perfect and they feel anxious if it isn't.

Identifying your dominant drivers

This exercise helps you to look at your dominant drivers, which may be impacting on how your plan and goal is progressing e.g., if you have a "be perfect" driver, you may be finding it hard to get things finished, or if you have a "hurry up" driver you may be thinking you are not going fast enough. All these patterns of behaviour may be holding you back. Building this self-awareness will help you to identify what you need to work on.

Look at the descriptions below and consider which sound most like you:

1) A – I usually manage everything on my own

    B – When I do things, I do them well

    C – I find it hard to say no

    D – I am usually moving and busy

    E – You have to put in the work to get results

2) A – I don't trust many people

    B – I don't like it when I see mistakes in other people's work

    C – I find myself nodding along to others

    D – I can interrupt others if I feel they are rambling

    E – I finish what I have started

3) A – I rarely take time off work and tend to plough through

    B – I can always see ways my work can be better

    C – I thrive on positive feedback from others

    D – I multi-task so I can get more done

    E – I always do my best

4) A – I rarely cry or show my emotions

B – I want to be the best

C – I worry people may not like me

D – I work at a fast pace

E – I don't give up, I know I can always do more

Mostly As - Be strong

Mostly Bs - Be perfect

Mostly Cs - Please others

Mostly Ds - Hurry up

Mostly Es - Try harder

Noticing your behaviours

After doing the drivers exercise, try to notice where you see these behaviours playing out – for example, if you scored high on "be perfect", notice when you might put off doing things because it is never the right time or you don't have all the details.

If you resonate with people-pleasing, you may notice that you avoid difficult conversations or situations where there may be conflict, or that you tell people that things are OK when they aren't, and instead let yourself fester.

A strong driver for me is "please others". I have often been so concerned about other people's feelings and keeping the peace that I have stayed in relationships for longer than I should, kept people employed for longer than I should have and stalled on making decisions or having difficult conversations.

Reflect on how you feel about the drivers you've discovered sabotaging you in moving toward your goals. All of us have drivers, so there is no shame here – it's time to be honest with yourself. Now you have the experience of making changes, you can begin to notice and work on the things that have been holding you back.

Self-compassion

Sometimes, things come along that we don't know how to deal with, pushing us out of our window of tolerance and making it difficult for us to move forward. If you are having a hard time and challenging things have been going on around you, revisit what you can and can't control and be compassionate to yourself.

Self-compassion is not only for when you are going through a difficult period; it is about being kind to yourself all the time. This is about silencing your inner critic and bigging up your inner cheerleader. It is an important part of building self-belief and keeping our motivation up, as sometimes things won't go to plan.

Self-compassion is made of three elements:

- **Kindness**: Consider how you can speak to yourself with kindness rather than judgement – for example, if you had an interview and didn't get the job, think about what you would say to yourself in a compassionate way – praising yourself for what you did well, rather than criticizing yourself for what you didn't do well.

- **Self-connection**: This is about being able to feel into your emotions and reflect on their roots. For example, if you have had an argument with a friend or family member, it is normal to feel upset. Allow yourself time to process your emotions and feelings. Negative feelings may also come up when you are implementing your

90-day plan – for example, if you go into your CEO meeting (see page 182) and feel you haven't made progress, you may be annoyed and angry with yourself – these emotions are all valid. Remind yourself that this is all part of the learning and that data I have spoken about.

- **Mindfulness**: This is about being present with yourself in the moment and exploring what is going on for you with a compassionate lens, acknowledging that whatever you are feeling or thinking is valid.

Looking at things through a lens of compassion allows you to think, "OK, there are some really big challenges for me right now, and I am feeling pretty stuck and a bit sad about what is going on. This is OK – it is normal to feel like this. What can I do to feel better and get some support?" rather than berating yourself: "There are some really big challenges for me right now and I am feeling pretty stuck and a bit sad. I should be able to find solutions and I need to stop feeling sad now and just get on with it."

I have had clients who have had significant illnesses or have lost loved ones suddenly and so, we have paused the coaching and the forward movement. Sometimes, treading water for a while is what you need to be able to swim ahead. This is why I encourage you to have CEO meetings each week, to reflect on where you are in your 90-day plan and review where you are going. At times, you may need to pause or change course and that is perfectly OK.

Remember, your progress is your progress. The only thing that will happen when you compare your progress to others is you will lose your joy, and we don't want that to happen!

KEY POINTS TO REMEMBER

- Step into a positive frame to move toward success.
- The power of mindset and self-belief will support your growth.
- Switch up your inner dialogue.
- Be aware of your window of tolerance.
- Your ego state can impact your relationships.
- Everyone has drivers and yours may slow your progress.
- Self-compassion is essential, always.

STEP FOUR

Integrate and Embed Change

In this section, you will discover how you integrate and ensure you stay moving toward your goal. Things may start well, but if you don't embed change it can feel demoralizing. On a neuroscience level, if we want lasting behavioural change, it needs to be programmed in the basal ganglia area in our brain (see page 3).

However, even if you fall off the wagon, you aren't necessarily going back to square one; keep in mind that you have already built the pathways in your brain and started the process, even if it hasn't been fully secured. If you consider this from a stimulus–response model, you can see if the response needs to be linked to the stimulus in the brain, which takes time and repetition. When you feel yourself going back to old behavioural patterns, remember you can see these as temporary and allow yourself to recalibrate back to what you want to achieve in the longer term.

The big questions that you will address in Step Four are:

- **How can you maximize the compound effect?** You will be exploring how to keep on track and continue to measure your progress against your goals.
- **What could be sabotaging your success?** You will be getting honest with yourself about boundaries and what is sabotaging your progress, and taking action to help you stay on track.
- **How can you continue to integrate?** You will be reflecting on how far you have come and what you need to go to the next level of you.

The compound effect

The way that we change often isn't dramatic. It is the small habits that we start to embed – walking instead of taking the bus, saying no to things rather than yes, the honest conversations that we have with ourselves and others. This is often known as the "compound effect". It is something James Clear talks about in his bestselling book *Atomic Habits* – if we can make a one per cent behavioural change every day over a year, that is significant.

When I am working with clients, we often go back to looking at the "perfect" behaviour or state to create a benchmark of what 10/10 looks and feels like for them. This can be valuable in providing that future state which they are working toward and can activate PEAs (positive emotional attractors), meaning that I am working more effectively with their brains, specifically in the prefrontal cortex and other areas where behavioural change occurs. Using this benchmark supports stepping into that bigger forward-focused vision. Then we look at the first step to move toward the bigger number. In some cases, this may be going from 2–2.5 out of 10.

If you aren't already using this benchmarking, have a go. It is a simple and effective way to start strengthening those neural pathways and embedding long-term behavioural change.

Honesty and authenticity

Now is the time to be honest and bold with those around you in a compassionate way. Clear is kind when it comes to relationships, friendships and at work. Not only do you feel happier when you are showing up this way, it means people know where they stand. You will be much more magnetic if you aren't playing games or holding onto resentment because you refuse to have conversations.

Equally, this is about being honest with yourself and taking responsibility. It is so easy to lay the blame on other people and get sucked into the drama cycle. Remember, we are all responsible for our own choices. This doesn't negate that some of us, due to our context, have fewer choices than others but when we choose it feels better.

When we do choose – make decisions – it is important that those decisions come from a place of alignment rather than fear. At times, we are all driven by fear and when our amygdala is activated and we go into our sympathetic nervous system (i.e. flight, fight or freeze mode), it takes energy away from our brain's command centre, the prefrontal cortex, where we think and make decisions. This is when we can feel stuck or make instinctive decisions that we regret at a later stage. It is the reason why I talk so much about doing the things that make you feel calm and connected to yourself. You are not going to make the right decisions or live a happy and fulfilled life if you are under high level of stress, causing a dysregulated nervous system.

One of the things which has made the biggest difference to me living an authentic and happy life is to be honest with those around me. We got to a stage in the business where our team was far too big – lots of people wanted to work with us, and I wanted to employ people as the people-pleaser element of my personality is really strong. After conversations with my accountant, I realized that our wage bill was way too high, coupled with the fact that we didn't have clear performance management processes. There were people I was paying a lot but weren't delivering. It was impacting the business and my own mental wellbeing. Having honest conversations with people, and looking at what we needed rather than what others told me, changed the organizational culture and improved our performance and our employees' happiness at work. These conversations weren't easy, but a couple of years later and our business is thriving with a cohesive team that has great relationships.

Moments of reflection

As you are committed to living a happier and more fulfilled life, it is useful to know and understand that everything may not always be smooth sailing. We all go through periods when things don't work out or when we need to press the pause button and slow down. Often, these periods of calm are an opportunity to reconnect with where we are and re-evaluate what we want to do. As we commit to making changes and moving forward toward new goals and desires, we may find that the things we thought we wanted have changed. That is why it is so important to give yourself space to reflect and integrate.

Like time, our energy is finite so a lot of this work revolves around you tuning in to how you are expending your energy; what is helping you ramp up your battery power and what is making you feel depleted. Using your energy as a baseline and tapping into what you need can be really useful when you are making decisions. See your energy as a compass, guiding you to decide what to do, who to spend time with and where to go next.

Your own path

The more you can let go of comparisons, self-judgement and the fear of being judged by others, and focus on what you really need and desire, the more you will feel at peace with yourself. If we go through life believing everyone is operating in their own way, with the premise that they are doing what they can to survive and thrive, we realize that most people are oblivious to us and our lives.

Commitment

This is about your commitment to yourself. You can go back and revisit any area of this book when you are feeling stuck or want to do something different. The model stays true: you assess where you are and what is going on, then get clear on your desires and where you want to be. You formulate your plan and strategy to move toward that future state, and then you take action and embed that action into your life. This model can be applied to whatever you are doing. And as visualizing your future state is energizing, this can often open up more possibilities cognitively than if you approach your plan from where you currently are.

Applying this framework to your life is a powerful way to self-coach yourself out of any situation; breaking down the plan into how you will work on your thoughts and emotions, alongside how you are showing up and what you are doing. Remember that the smallest steps done frequently lead to the longest lasting sustainable changes.

STEP FOUR AIMS

- Learn how to establish clear boundaries and say no to what doesn't serve you.
- Discover how boundaries can bring you more of what you desire.
- Step out of the comparison trap.
- Let go of self-judgement and judgement of others.
- Build your plan for long-term success and happiness.

10

Boundaries and Motivations

If you want to achieve what is important to you, then it is time to get clear on your boundaries and what is and isn't going to help you. If you are constantly chasing your tail, putting other people's needs before your own and saying yes to everything, I can guarantee you will soon reach exhaustion and burnout. It is essential to meet your own needs and to know your limitations.

I know about burnout only too well ... I have been there physically, emotionally and cognitively, rushing around to support others, spending hours on the phone and being unable to switch off. I was left so drained, which made me realize there must be another way.

In this chapter, you will explore:

- How saying no means you are putting your desires first
- How to create and enforce boundaries
- Dealing with people who push those boundaries
- Accepting that you can only be happy if you are sometimes selfish

Often, my clients come to me on the verge of burnout: they are juggling multiple responsibilities and finding it hard to see the wood from the trees. By working together, I support them to identify what they want to keep hold of and what they want to let go of, and to start to build and develop more effective boundaries, so they have more space and less overwhelm.

If you really want to live the life of your dreams and aren't moving forwards, then you need to have difficult conversations, both with yourself and with others. It starts with you: explore how you can set boundaries and give yourself more space. It might be that you committed to something when you could have said no, or that there are things which you need to consider and work through in order to honour your commitments. If you have already signed up to something, it can be difficult to go back to people, but you need to be honest about your capabilities and limitations, and realize that the discomfort of the conversation will be worth it in the long term.

Bandwidth and multitasking

You can only do so many things at a time. In 2015, researchers at University College London (UCL) looked at how multitasking impacts our cognitive abilities and found it had a detrimental effect on productivity and performance. As it was based on office-style work and these are usually work-related behaviours, they were seen as less harmful, but these effects were also seen in contexts such as driving, which is extremely dangerous! This is one of the reasons why, in the UK, it is now illegal to talk on the phone whilst driving: cognitively our reactions are not as fast because our brain is running much slower due to the multiple demands placed on it.

You only have a certain amount of bandwidth or headspace. If you multitask, you diminish your executive function and cognition – you basically make yourself less smart, reducing your ability to solve problems, think creatively or do things differently. Alongside the cognitive impacts, multitasking can have an emotional impact. I have witnessed people having an emotional response to notifications on their phone. Unless you're working in a vital role that requires you to be always contactable (such as the emergency services), you don't need to have notifications on and you certainly don't need to know the moment "Sophie has uploaded a photo" onto social media!

Whenever you decide to multitask, you're deciding to do things to a lower standard and increase your stressors. Is this something you want to do? About eight years ago, I did some work with Brendon Burchard, a motivational speaker and coach, who is obsessed with high performance habits. One of the key takeaways from this work was to create time for "chunks" of work each day without distraction: phones away, all programs closed down and a timer. Brendon suggested up to 50-minute chunks. I prefer to do 30-minute sprints where I have that complete focus. In these times, I make sure I only have one tab open and I set an alarm. Doing this focused work is how I wrote this book. After 30 minutes, I give myself a "brain break", which usually involves going outside or making a drink. Sometimes I dance or do star jumps and then I come back to my next task.

How boundary setting impacts your wellbeing

Do you want to be happier? There is evidence that setting boundaries helps reduce our cognitive and emotional loads and therefore enables us to be happier, think more clearly and make better decisions. Equally, when we set boundaries, we are taking back control of how we spend our time. When we feel we have more control and autonomy over our lives, we feel happier.

You may also want to consider what boundaries are imposed on you. We are likely to have organizational and societal constraints, based on a set of rules, requirements or ways of behaving. Depending on how compliant we are, and our need for certainty, we may find these more helpful or unhelpful.

SCARF model

The neuroscientist, David Rock's SCARF model, as trademarked by the NeuroLeadership Institute, works on the premise that you are always moving toward reward and away from threat. You'll have a preference for a different blend of the model's ingredients, which relate to:

S – Status and how we compare ourselves to others
C – Certainty
A – Autonomy
R – Relatedness
F – Fairness or equity

These questions are based on my interpretation of each category, to help you determine your preferences:

Status
Tick all those that apply to you:
- I compare myself to others frequently
- It is important for me to be seen and heard by others
- I worry about what others think of me

The more you have ticked, the more STATUS is important to you.

Certainty

Tick all those that apply to you:

- I like to know what is going to happen next
- At work, I like processes and systems to follow
- I feel happiest when I can predict the future

The more you have ticked, the more CERTAINITY is important to you.

Autonomy

Tick all those that apply to you:

- I like to do things when I choose
- I find it hard when people tell me what to do
- I have a need to be in control

The more you have ticked, the more AUTONOMY is important to you.

Relatedness

Tick all those that apply to you:

- I like to feel connected to others
- Relationships are important to me
- I want to be liked

The more you have ticked, the more RELATEDNESS Is important to you.

Fairness

Tick all those that apply to you:

- It is important to me that everyone is treated the same
- I get upset when I feel things aren't fair
- I speak up when I think something is not fair

> The more you have ticked, the more FAIRNESS is important to you.
>
> We all have a need for each of these elements in different amounts. From doing this exercise and your own assessment, consider which of these are most significant for you and start to recognize how this might influence your behaviour.

Setting your own boundaries

By understanding your preferences, through doing exercises such as the SCARF model, you can start to recognize what is important to you and consider how you can set boundaries to support that. For example, If you're high on certainty, you may respond well to boundaries as they help you to understand what behaviours are expected of you and it may feel safer to have processes and rules. By contrast, if you're high on autonomy, you may find strict boundaries more challenging as you may see them as a threat to your freedom. This is because we all have preferences: what works for someone else may not be the most effective thing for you.

When I use the SCARF model with clients, we spend most of our time looking at how they can move toward a positive outcome, rather than away from the perceived threat. This is because coaching is positive and forward focused – the move toward positivity is supported by the brain's dopamine response, which helps to embed change, allowing the client to think more effectively.

Boundary theory – work/life boundaries

This psychological theory looks at how people create, maintain and even change boundaries so they are able to classify and simplify what is going on around them[19]. Our brains are always looking for ways to make connections between different pieces of information, so we can create rules, which help us to navigate what is going on around us.

Boundary theory looks at:

- **Cognitive**: this relates to how you think and interact with others – for example, you might set a boundary to not speak about specific topics with someone.
- **Physical**: this relates to your what you eat and drink and when you're active or resting, as well as your body and your space. For example, you might set a boundary saying you only eat organic food, or that you go to bed at 10pm each night.
- **Behavioural**: this relates to how you act and the rules you want others to follow – for example, you might set a boundary where you say you won't go to office drinks as you don't drink alcohol.

Boundaries between work and life help signify the differences between the two domains; the way that you behave and the rules of engagement at work and home tend to be different. Thick boundaries refer to when things are kept separate – for example, you might choose to work in a different location to where you live, or these may be more blended as you work and live in the same space.

Since working from home has increased in prevalence over the last few years, it is has become clear that many of our thick boundaries have become thin or even non-existent, and we have lost many of the micro-transitions that signified the movement from one domain to another – for example, the physical commute or the putting on of our work "uniform". The lack of boundaries between work and home can result in increased stress levels in the home, which impacts family relationships. For example, if you are working from your kitchen table and have had a bad day at work, when you then eat your evening meal at the same table you are entering back into that physically stressful environment, which can make you feel cognitively stressed as well. This can lead to sympathetic nervous system activation and a fight, flight, freeze or fawn response.

In my coaching sessions, I am working with more and more clients who are finding that they are unable to create boundaries between work and life, sometimes amplified by flexible working. One of the first steps can be looking at creating physical boundaries. For example, when working from home:

- Having a designated workspace, garden office or office can help you cognitively and emotionally keep work "separate".
- Using a desktop rather than a laptop can support this boundary of difference.
- Creating micro-transitions between work and home – for example, going for a walk around the block before and after work, or changing into different clothes.
- Having a work phone, which you switch off when not "at work".

The more you can create physical boundaries between work and life, the more you can establish emotional and cognitive boundaries and not bring work stressors into the home and vice versa.

Setting boundaries with yourself and others

First you need to set boundaries with yourself. One of the ways that I work with clients on boundaries is to have them imagine that they are in a place where they have clear, firm boundaries and to think about how they feel, what they are thinking and what is going on around them. This mini visualization often leads to them writing down and committing to their boundaries.

Part of setting boundaries is about saying: "This isn't going to work for me". I invite my coaching clients to consider these "rules" as best practice and imagine that they can be a simple way to aid decision-making. If you feel that rules are too rigid, consider them as operational guidelines which can be flexible depending on how you feel and what you desire in a situation. The key is to remember you are in control.

Setting boundaries

When we looked at the SCARF model (see page 216), you would have learnt that you had a need for certain things in your life. In order to help meet those needs and the needs that you discovered during our work on Maslow in Step One (see page 67), it is important to set boundaries. This exercise can support you to do this.

Reflect on the following:
- What do you want to feel?
- What do you want to be thinking?
- What do you want to be doing?
- How do you want to be showing up?

Now consider what you need to make this happen. You might think:

I want to feel calm. To do this, I need to create more space for me in my day. I need to say no to things which make me feel stressed, like driving during rush hour.

I want to feel confident. To do this I need ...

And so on.

Now complete this for you:

I want to feel ...
To do this I need ...

I want to be thinking ...
To do this I need ...

I want to be doing ...
To do this I need ...

I want to be showing up as ...
To do this I need ...

Use your reflections to work out what you need to say no to, and what your boundaries may look like.

Work boundaries

I saw some great boundary setting by one of my mentors when I was a deputy head teacher. My mentor was a highly experienced deputy with a young daughter. She was excellent at her job and someone all of us went to for advice and guidance. She was also very clear on her working hours: she would be at work by 8:15/8:30am and would leave at 4:30/5pm. She did some work at home, once her daughter was in bed, however she drew a line in the sand and said these are my boundaries to protect her time with her daughter. The modelling of working hours and commitments was inspiring for me. I was delighted to see her voted Head Teacher of the Year recently – a testament to the fact that strong boundaries don't impact your success!

Personal boundaries

It can be difficult to set boundaries with those who are close to us – for example, if you usually socialize and drink alcohol with your friend and then decide to have time away from alcohol, it may make your friend feel insecure as they start to reflect on their own relationship with alcohol.

If you apply the SCARF model (see page 216) to relationships, there is an unconscious comparison of status. If you set a boundary, it can change this dynamic for the other person, which may put them into threat mode as they feel insecure. For example, if you always answer the phone to your mum, however busy you are, and then decide to put in boundaries about when you can speak to her, it may make her feel that she is less important to you. That is why it is so important to communicate the boundary and the reasons behind it. For example, by telling her that your work is really busy during the day so the best time you can speak to her is from 6–8pm, rather than just not answering your phone. As always, communication is key.

A great perspective when setting boundaries is to focus on the gains and rewards from having them in place. This works with the brain's reward centre, as you are anticipating pleasure and that helps you to embed the boundary. Equally, focusing on your vision for who you want to become and what you want to do can help you to refocus on the positive when you have these conversations.

It's important to consider why you are setting the boundary and what you will gain from this. Step into that confident, assertive version of yourself when you are doing this, linking it in with your big vision (see page xx) from Step Two and how this will help you achieve that vision.

Building the "no" muscle

One simple way to set boundaries is to say no more. We have been conditioned to believe that saying yes is positive, and saying no will shut down possibilities and opportunities, or appear rude or selfish. When you say no to something, you are being clear about what is important to you and reinforcing your boundaries.

The word "no" seems to be one of the most feared words in our language and although "no" is a complete sentence, it can feel uncomfortable to use it, as it feels very direct and abrupt. You can soften this by considering how you phrase your "no". For example, you might say, "I am really sorry but that is not a priority right now" or "I have a lot on and don't have the bandwidth". Due to my work, I get a lot of people wanting to "pick my brains" or have some of my time. My response is always honest – "I work around my family and although this can result in evening and weekend training sessions, I do my best not to book anything else in as they are my priority" or "Here is the link to pay for a 'pick my brains' call".

Like anything, practice makes perfect so start to flex your "no" muscle and practise saying it in everyday situations. For example, if you are someone who may be tempted by the upsell, the next time you are in Starbucks and are asked if you want anything else, say no. The more that you practise, the more that you will build a strong neural pathway. Remember, this easy no is the start of flexing that no muscle. If you find this too straightforward, give yourself a bigger challenge – for example, by saying no to that extra glass of wine or episode of Netflix, or that third night out in a week, which you know will make you tired and grumpy.

Of course, you need to respect how others respond to your boundaries and the way that you present them. Be kind and compassionate, especially when you're delivering news that may be upsetting or uncomfortable for them. For example, if you're telling a friend that you don't want to spend as much time with them, or you are telling your boss that you aren't doing the "extra" work they gifted you, their reaction may not be positive. Before you have these conversations, ground yourself by remembering that the only thing you can control is you, and that you are doing this so you can be a happier and better person around those you love.

Setting boundaries with others

When you have this set of "organizing principles", you can use it to make better decisions and ensure that you have an internal compass which allows you to say "yes" or "no" to things. I find having a written set of "rules", which have firm reasons behind them, allows me to step away from the personal side of decision-making and ensure it is more logical – for example, I only travel into London a maximum of twice a week because I know I can feel depleted if I do more. Knowing why I do this helps me to manage my time and plan more effectively.

It is great to know your boundaries and have the confidence to assert them when needed. You often need to verbalize them as well. By doing this, you're being clear about your needs and you're also inviting other people to accept them. Remember, you can't control whether people will accept them so see this as an invite and if you are serious about changing your life, you will have to reaffirm them.

A positive way to present boundaries is to give reasons for why you are putting them in place and perhaps offer a compromise – for example, "I can't continue to do this as it is impacting my energy levels and I am feeling overwhelmed. What I can do is xxx. How does that sound?" This approach allows people to understand your thinking and can be a softer way of being assertive. Of course, if you prefer, you can say "no" without offering an explanation or compromise.

Time boundaries

Imagine what you would be doing if you could have full autonomy over how you spend your time.

In reality, many of us have certain responsibilities – for example, if we have caring responsibilities, employees or businesses, we have to do certain things to keep others alive, keep our employees happy and earn money! Depending on these circumstances, it may mean we have more or less time autonomy.

Our boundaries around time can be highly personal and can make a huge difference to how we feel. By creating time boundaries, we are exerting our preferences and "value tagging" to our brains what is important to us. When you looked at values in Step One, you will have discovered what is important to you by how you spend your time.

I am strict about having three set times a week for exercise – my personal trainer, a gym session and a Pilates class. These are booked in my diary months in advance and, unless I have an event, I don't miss them. I know these help me look and feel better, and mean I am more productive. I say no to anything that impacts these and my calendar is set up in such a way that no one can book anything else in.

A lot of the work I do with clients is around planning, boundaries and the elusive work/life balance. By mapping out on paper what they want and then putting structures in place to ensure these things happen, they often feel more in control and their stress and overwhelm decreases. I love to ask them "What are you no longer available for and then how will you commit to this?" I would love for you to reflect on these questions too.

The perfect week

Within your current context, consider what your perfect week would look like in terms of how you spend your time. What would your days look like? Complete the example below.

- Wake up:
- Morning routine/activities:
- Lunchtime:
- Afternoon activities:
- Dinner:
- Evening activities:

Consider how this schedule would make you feel.
What would you like to be doing more of?
What would you like to be doing less of?

Now consider the week:
- What would you like to do each day?
- How would you like your week to feel?

- What would you like to do more of?
- What would you like to do less of?

Now, reflect on what you have written and consider what elements of this you can bring into your life.

Are boundaries selfish?

People often tell me they find boundaries difficult because they think it is selfish behaviour, but being selfish is sometimes important. In a previous business, I got into a position where I was putting my employees before myself. I even skipped paying myself a couple of times. Now, this was not a good nor sustainable place to be. As the business owner, I needed to earn money otherwise the business would go under. After a conversation with my accountant, coach and a sharp talking to myself, I realized that what I was doing was incredibly harmful to the whole business, and made decisions which secured our long-term success and meant I was being paid!

A famous saying I have is, "Who is looking after you?" and then "Who is looking after them?" I say this a lot to friends who are going through hard times. It is so important that we all have our needs cared for, otherwise we fall over. The strong friend who is always there for you – who is picking them up? Think about it.

This is about really looking at what you need and being bold enough to go for it. It doesn't mean you need to tread on anyone or be mean. It means being honest. Saying I can't do this as I have commitments is OK. Some people will prefer you not to have boundaries as this version of you may mean that they are not able to do what they want. Remember, this

BOUNDARIES AND MOTIVATIONS

response does not consider your needs and if people around you don't want you to be truly happy, maybe it is worth choosing your companions more wisely. This can be harder if the person is family or someone you work closely with but remember that you can only control how you respond to others and your behaviour. If people choose not to interact with your boundaries, that is their prerogative.

Part of the problem is what we have been conditioned to believe about being selfish. I remember reading an article by Polly Vernon, a journalist, in which she talked about her choice not to have children and she said that it was a selfish choice – I loved the way she wrote this and it really rings true on so many levels. Surely, we would be living in a much more functional world if all women were able to make their own "selfish" choice about if they wanted to be a mother, rather than feeling like it was a rite of passage that they had to take.

When people push boundaries

I find it interesting when people push boundaries, especially when I have been clear on what they are. For example, I might tell someone that I am unavailable at a certain time and then get an influx of messages from them at this time. The person may be unconsciously pushing the boundaries. I have had people phone me or send me "urgent" emails when I am off, including on my children's birthdays, which can be really frustrating. When your brain's threat centre is activated, it can be hard not to react. Reminding yourself to take a step away so you can respond rather than react is useful here.

If you check emails on holiday or out of hours, that is a choice you are making. If your employer expects a reply, then this is different – it is about the intention behind the behaviour and the cultural norms of the organisation. If an employer expects out-of-hours work or something when you are on holiday, this is something you need to discuss with them. Occasionally, it may be that they need something but that should be infrequent.

If people in your personal life push boundaries, it is best to raise this with them – for example, if a friend or family member often turns up unannounced at your house and this is something you don't like, say something like, "When you turn up, it can make me feel stressed. It would be helpful if you let me know you are coming". The more we can communicate our needs and boundaries, the more we can build adult relationships which help us to feel happier.

Finally, remember that when people push boundaries it tends to be because they see the world through their lens. Your changing behaviour may have an impact on them that they don't like. A classic example is when people decide to stop drinking alcohol. Often, especially at the start, they may want to change their behaviour by avoiding pubs and bars. If you are the friend who still wants to go out and drink, you can understand why you might feel a bit aggrieved as you feel that you have lost something. If you are in a situation like this, start with compassion and support for what is important to your friends. Using the example above, accept that the person still enjoys drinking alcohol and going to pubs. When we stop deciding how others should behave, and instead focus on ourselves, we feel more relaxed. We can never control others – all we can do is control ourselves.

Energy and boundaries

When you set boundaries, what you're really doing is protecting your energy. You know that some people make you feel good and upbeat and some people drag you down. Often, this is about how well we get on with people and what they have going on. A friend who only moans or talks about themselves constantly is probably not a great energetic match and if you are mindful of how you feel, it might be worth reducing the time you spend with them.

Being aware of what takes your energy can help you identify how you want to spend your time and who you want to spend it with. I remove myself from situations where there is drama or people talking negatively about others. I know that this type of energy drains me and impacts how I feel about myself.

In my experience, when you have thin, or soft boundaries, your energy is always the thing that goes. You may notice your sparkle has dimmed or that you start to hold onto resentment for others. If you feel like you're the person who has to "do everything", it may well be a sign that your boundaries are too flexible.

If you feel like you need a rest when you come away from certain situations or people, take some time to reflect on how you can protect your energy in the future – for example, can you meet the friend who drains you, but you want to stay loyal to, in a group instead? If you know you never feel good after going to your work's Christmas party, can you say no to attending this year (hint – yes you can)? If you want to live a happier life, then being in tune with and mapping your energy flows makes a huge difference.

Mapping your energy

After you've spent time with someone or been somewhere, ask yourself:
- How does this make me feel?
- How does this help me achieve what is important to me?

If it isn't positive, it is time to reflect and move on. You don't need to be miserable or live your life based on other people's agendas. True success and happiness come from living your life by your standards, rather than bending over backwards to fit into someone else's way of doing things. The more that you recognize this, the more it can encourage you to be mindful of where you are expending energy and where your energy is being drained.

A common piece of advice I have heard repeated time and time again is that you need to upgrade your friends to be successful. As someone who has known the bulk of my friends for over 20 years, I don't agree. I do think we need to check in on who we personally find toxic for our energy. I don't believe that people are "toxic", but that some behaviours are toxic and some combinations of people can become energy draining.

For most of my adult life, I have held onto a pretty stable group of friends and it has been pretty drama free. Of course, like the tides, friendships can ebb and flow. Since I started working online, I found that there were so many "in gangs" and toxic behaviours, which deeply unsettled me and took me back to being bullied at school. I felt this in my body and my perceived threat response was sounding very loudly in my brain. The first time I experienced it I "fought" and stood up for myself, which only caused pain on both sides. As I started to realize that there was nothing positive to gain from being in these conflicts, I stepped out of the drama and found a community of others who I now meet with regularly.

I was able to do this by calming my nervous system when I felt I was being activated. For me this stimulus–response behaviour included removing myself from situations, doing breathing exercises to recalibrate and then journalling or reflecting on what I felt and finding a way forward. In effect, I do a mini self-coaching exercise, which enables me to think more clearly and confidently about what is going on for me.

I'm sharing this because it is important to realize that in every situation you can find people who you resonate with. Those who are happiest tend to be those who are avoiding the drama and blame, and getting on with their own stuff. These are the people I encourage you to spend time with; people who build you up and make you feel good because, as you know, life can be short – let's make it fun along the way.

Beyond self-care

On Instagram, you often see memes about putting on you own life jacket first or practicing self-care. It's easy to mock these, but they have an element of truth. In reality, you do need to put yourself first – you do need to prioritize your needs. I've put myself in situations where I've convinced myself that I will start looking after myself tomorrow. I will start exercising tomorrow. I will delegate that tomorrow. I will ask for help ... The more that we allow ourselves to be beholden to what other people need, without thinking about ourselves, the more we deplete our own lives.

If you want to achieve your goals and feel good, you need to look after yourself. Working hard for a deadline can feel productive and motivating. In the short-term, this may not have any negative effects but in the long-term, it can mean that you're pushing yourself really hard every day and aren't giving yourself space to relax and reset, meaning you will likely become ill or burnt out. Ask yourself "What do I need today to thrive?" and then "How will doing this now help the future version of me?"

REFLECTION

Journal using the following questions as prompts:
- What do I need to thrive every day?
- What do I need each week to thrive?
- What do I need each month?
- When am I at my best?
- What can I do to support me to feel this way?
- What support do I need to ensure this happens?

Motivation

It is only natural for your motivation to take a few dips along the way. Life can get in the way and it may well be that the change you desire is taking longer than expected. Simon Sinek, motivational speaker, says "start with why". Checking in regularly with "why" can help you to stay motivated when things are tough.

Your motivation to change needs to be stronger than your desire to stay where you are. As you continue to move toward your goal, your brain may decide that where you are is "fine", or you may find your progress has plateaued. At this point, it is so easy to settle back into old habits or to decide it is too hard. That is why we talk about the compound effect and the fact that you can build through small steps every day, rather than huge ones all at once.

If you're finding you are making progress when you do your weekly CEO meetings (see page 182), how are you rewarding that? Are you treating yourself or indulging in something that brings you pleasure? The key here is to make sure the reward fits the goal – for example, if you are working on your physical health, your reward might be a massage, a relaxing bath or a foot soak – something which helps enhance your physical health, rather than eating a family bar of chocolate or drinking a bottle of wine.

One of my clients was struggling to move forward. We looked at rewards and she created a star chart to celebrate her progress. Her exact words were "Like I am five years old!" Guess what? The chart worked and this was just a "start" chart; seeing the stars add up each week was a motivator in itself. When we reward ourselves, we get that dopamine hit, which helps us to continue to practise the behaviour and strengthen those neural pathways.

Peaks and troughs in motivation or falling off the wagon doesn't mean you have failed. The falls are not what is important; it is how quickly you get back up. Notice how you speak to yourself at those times and be your own cheerleader. When we create new ways of thinking, feeling, being and doing in our brains, the old neural pathways remain there so we can return to old habits. Remind yourself that this is your brain taking it easy.

If you are low on motivation, revisiting the vision activities (see Chapter 4) can help inspire you. They help you tap back into the big picture thinking and positive emotion, which can activate those PEAs (see page 85) and open up creative thinking. You may realize you need to press pause and allow yourself time to integrate and reflect. Remember this is about living better and feeling better, so the only person who sets the pace is you.

KEY POINTS TO REMEMBER

- Clear is kind – setting boundaries helps you focus on what is important.
- Being selfish gives you more time and energy for those you love and care about.
- Start to build your "no" muscle.
- People who don't like your boundaries are operating from their place of lack.
- Your energy is one of your superpowers – be mindful of it and how it is impacted by others.
- Be aware that your motivation may waiver and this is normal – create small rewards and celebrate your wins.

11

Stepping out of Judgement and Comparison

When I coach clients, two things I notice that stop them from moving forward are judgement and comparison.

In this chapter, you will explore:

- How you can reframe comparison and use it positively
- Where judgement comes from and what it can show us
- How happy people don't hurt others
- How compassion for yourself and others makes a difference in life
- How your views on being nice may be blocking your happiness

Comparison

Nothing good ever came from comparing yourself to someone else. Many people are in the habit of doing this, looking at how they "measure up" from an early age and internalizing this idea that they need to make a comparison. It probably comes partly from school, where we are made aware of where we are in comparison to others (most kids can tell what "table" they are on by who else is on it).

After I had my first daughter, I had a great group of friends who I met at antenatal classes. I spent a lot of time comparing my post-baby weight to theirs and found I was measuring my value by my weight. Although I have never been super-skinny, I definitely felt "lesser" as I wasn't as small. Looking back, I wish I had spent my time embracing who I was and the beautiful human I had created, instead of worrying about whether my thighs looked bigger than everyone else's.

My comparison journey hasn't always been about my appearance; it has been about my intelligence, my income, my happiness. You name it, I have compared it and I have spent hours of my life (probably years) where I have felt lacking. Comparison has made me feel like I don't measure up and it has made me judge myself harshly, and the sad truth is that it has not done anything to make me feel good or like myself any better. It has stopped me from doing things and it has made me waste time.

And I am sure I am not alone.

It is so easy to compare yourself to others and find yourself wanting – and here is the thing, we don't ever really know what is going on in people's lives. My beautiful friend with glamorous Instagram photos struggles with loneliness and anxiety. The friend who posts her "perfect life" is plagued by her partner's infidelity. The businesswoman who posts about money and what she has achieved is working 24/7.

You get the picture. We compare our back of house with other people's front of house. In fact, it has become so normal to only present the best version of yourself that when people are open, honest and vulnerable about elements of their life on social media, they often get a negative reaction.

When I shared about my anxiety, people offered me "fixes" to make me anxiety-free. As someone who has done a lot of therapy, coaching and everything else, I understand what triggers my anxiety and what exactly I need. I just wanted to show that perfect doesn't exist as a way of supporting others to open up to their vulnerabilities, and that humans are fallible.

Remember, our best lives, our happy lives and our fulfilled lives may also be messy. We may not be looking at the camera in our photos, we may not live in the biggest house or have the best body and that is OK.

With all the comparison, there will be people looking up to you and want what you have, and who see you as someone who has the life they want. Only you truly know how you think and feel, and how happy or unhappy you are.

What comparison can show us

Comparison is only useful as a way to highlight what you really want. What is it that others have that you want? Look at comparison as a clue to what you desire, rather than allowing you to be wanting, and then think about how this will translate into your life. Comparison and desire are the clues; you need to make it work for you and your life. Let that insight drive your inner compass.

REFLECTION

If you feel comparison creeping up, reflect on the following questions:

- What can I learn from this?
- How is this signaling my desires?
- What will I do as a result of feeling this?

When you frame comparison as a way to value tag what is important, it can be a positive experience and motivational. You may find it useful to go back to your vision board if you feel drawn to particular things that others have, so you can ensure that they are consistent with what you want. I truly believe that we can take cues from what is activating us or making us feel envious, and use it for good.

Judgement

If you're going to live your best life and step into the power of who you are, you need to let go of judgement. The more you judge others and yourself, the more you're giving away your power energetically and staying small.

A saying that is common in the personal development space is "happy people don't hurt people". What this means is if someone is being negative, unkind or cruel, it is likely to be based on how they are feeling rather than a reflection of you. Having spent seven years in the online business world, I would say there are a fair few unhappy people.

I once wrote a post about how personal development had really helped me to change my life and become more confident, and how it led me to meet my now husband. The story was one of hope and my intention was it for to be inspirational. I wrote it whilst on a plane back from Australia and when I landed at Abu Dhabi, the comments had started "this is an awful post, you are pathetic saying you need a man to be happy" etc. I remember sitting in the airport with tears streaming down my face, thinking what is making this person hate me?

And here is the thing, you may be reading this book and you might not like me. In fact, you may be judging me. I can't control that nor can I make you like me (I wish my 12-year-old self had realized this!). However, I know your judgement will be coming directly from you as there will be something you see in me which either:

- You wish you had
- Reminds you of someone you don't like
- You also see in yourself but don't like

One of my closest friends is the most beautiful, engaging, intelligent woman you will ever meet, with a huge heart like a lion. At times, she can be overwhelming and dominate conversations. You know why I judge her? Because I am aware that this is something I also do. I don't like that part of me, so I judge that part of her. I am self-aware enough to laugh at myself when I see these behaviours and realize what is going on, which means I can let go of the feelings that I have and see my friend for all her positives.

When you start to look at judgement as a direct result of what you are feeling about yourself, you start to see things in a different light – for example, I really struggled with an old friend who was sleeping with the boyfriends of other people that we knew. Then, I got myself into a situation where I did something very similar. It is not one of my proudest moments and something I wish I could have erased due to the pain it caused. The lesson there for me was clear – it is so easy to judge others when we aren't in their situation.

When I find myself judging someone and thinking "I would never do that", I check myself. We would all love to think we are above certain behaviours (wasn't this why *The Jeremy Kyle Show* was so popular), but until you walk in someone else's shoes, you can never truly know how they made their decisions. I strongly believe that the majority of people are doing the best they can in the circumstances they are in, and spending our time judging their behaviour is not going to make us happier or more fulfilled.

REFLECTION

Consider these questions if you find yourself judging others:
- How am I making this value judgement?
- What do I know is true?
- How do I feel about this person/situation?
- What else could be going on?
- How does this reflect what is going on in my life?
- What do I want to do about these feelings?

Compassion

One thing that helps with judgement, including self-judgement, is compassion. It is something I often bring to my clients' attention. One of my clients was going through a really tough time in her personal life and she was concerned about how this was affecting her work. When I reflected back to her that what she was dealing with was pretty significant, it gave her permission to go easy on herself and she was then able to move forward and refocus on her work.

Compassion starts with you: when you are compassionate toward yourself, it allows you to get rid of feelings of shame. Equally, when you practise compassion and kindness toward yourself, you are more likely to practise it toward others. Being kind does not mean being a pushover – it means being clear and, in my world, it means being direct.

We should learn to be self-compassionate, even when we get things wrong. I recently let go of someone and they were incredibly defensive and rude. In the end, I think I sunk to their level.

I'm sharing that experience as it is so important to be aware that sometimes you won't feel love and light and, when difficult emotions have been triggered, you may well react, not respond. For example, if you see someone attacking your child, your reaction will be instinctive and fuelled by adrenaline. Your reactions are there to tell you something and sometimes other people's behaviour does elicit a strong response.

This is about being compassionate and kind *most* of the time and when you are, even those small acts of kindness help you feel better. The small acts make a difference – smiling at people, saying hello, buying someone an extra coffee, doing the shopping for your elderly neighbour.

Nice people don't last

There is this idea that if you're nice, you come last. I don't believe that. I think being nice, with boundaries, means you sleep well at night. Whilst I go by one of my closest friend's life rules of "don't be a d*ck", I do believe being clear is kind and that being direct is not aggressive. You can be nice and want the best for people, and still look out for yourself.

Being "nice" does not need to mean you are a pushover. I have regularly been told I am too nice, but I have also been called a bully and a b***h. The reason I share that is because it is proof that it depends on your perspective! I think I am more on the nice side, with most of my close friends and family describing me as kind, although the projection of this to others may not always be visible.

Stepping out of the negative thinking cycle

We talked about our negative thought patterns earlier. Unfortunately, they don't just disappear. If you consider your inner critic's role is to keep you psychologically and physically safe, when you do something that your brain flags as "unsafe" (perhaps it is something new), you may find yourself stepping into that negative chatter. So, what can you do?

The first thing is to recognize it and, when you do, to remind yourself of how far you have come. The second thing is to change the dialogue. A good technique is to ask yourself "What evidence do I have that this is true?" or "How can I think differently about this?"

We can all sink into our "I am not good enough" pit at times. Modern life throws things at us and, sometimes, decisions that we make in the moment don't work out, people let us down and we can feel like we are walking through treacle.

There is a saying that the breakthrough comes after the breakdown, and that is something that I attest to. I remember being so close to losing everything: I'd made a series of bad investments, had taken out a loan with some shocking interest and had a job that I hated. My commute took me two hours a day, my dad, who was an alcoholic, was refusing treatment and drinking himself into an early grave. I was stuck in survival mode and going through the motions. One of my best friends told me to leave my job so I did and got a much better paid one, as well as doing some tutoring and other bits on the side. I got out of the hole as I saw a glimmer of hope and realized I could beat myself up all day long or move on.

The only person who is impacted by the way you talk to yourself is you, and the only person who can change it is you. If you have let yourself get into a spiral, start to reflect on where you are now and the progress you have made. Use the dating yourself principle mentioned previously and remind yourself that these old thought patterns and behaviours are easy to slip back into. The strength is in pulling yourself out of them, and ensuring that you don't make them too significant.

If you are going through a period of change, remind yourself that these thoughts becoming louder is part of the process, and acknowledge what they are showing you – that the path you are walking is the right one for you.

Making better decisions and challenging your thinking

This is about challenging you to think differently and step out of the unhelpful thought patterns that are stopping you from moving forward. I always say that we make decisions based on the information that we have in that moment; sometimes, we find out new information which changes our decisions.

Coaches help people challenge their thinking and look at things from different viewpoints. Being able to change your mind and your thinking is a sign that you are open-minded, and as long as you are consistent with your values and are not being influenced, it is a sign of learning and progress.

Why is this relevant here? Because as you embed these new habits and change how you think, you may well start to realize that some of your old decision-making came from a place of lack or a place of judgement, or that you have become overly reliant on one way of thinking and are not tuning into other perspectives and your cognitive flexibility.

Adam Grant, economist and author, examined the thinking of CEOs and leaders, and found that those who were the most successful allowed themselves to be wrong. They looked at ways to challenge what they thought and were creative in their approach to problem-solving. This is about having a flexible approach and allowing yourself to be wrong when presented with new information. It always comes back to the premise that we make decisions based on the information that we have available to us at the time. How great would it be if we lived in a world where everyone was confident enough to admit when they got something wrong?

In his TED talk, cognitive scientist Tom Griffin shares how to make decisions like a computer. He says that when we think in a logical way, our decisions are right 37 per cent of the time. By applying this to our own decision-making abilities, if we are around this mark, we are doing pretty well. Allowing ourselves to get things wrong, or change our minds when we have new information, cannot only enhance decision-making skills – it can also support the development of our growth mindset.

Great leaders often combine rational, logical thinking with their intuition, which can help them make more impactful decisions. This ability to consider what things feel like, as well as the facts, can be useful when you are looking at your goals, and can help you to explore what is working well and what is not working so well. You can then ask yourself, how can I learn from this?

Positive vibes, not toxic vibes

This is a reminder that although we know being able to reframe negative thoughts into positive ones is helpful, and seeing the learning in situations can help us to move forward, living a better life is not about always being like Pollyanna. Sometimes, things will be tough and when you are committed to living better, you need to acknowledge this.

If you are dealing with a difficult situation, your wellbeing and mental health may be impacted. If you are finding it hard to focus or look forward with optimism, or you are struggling with being in a consistent low mood, it is important to get support.

Connecting into the positive and the learning doesn't mean you will always be happy. It means you will feel better generally and be able to work through those hard things. Recognizing that hard times are temporary can be incredibly useful, and can help you to move forward as well.

You know that stress and cortisol impact your brain and your thinking, so when you have a difficult situation give yourself space to process and minimize the pressure you put on yourself to make decisions. It's easy to default to our preferred stress responses – mine is to do more and pack my diary. Over the years, I have done a lot of work on this and now make sure I build in even more rest if I feel stressed.

Putting in place rituals and habits to support yourself is important because when things are tough, these can have the biggest impact. If you have fallen out of the habit, take a step back and remind yourself what you need and what feels good. The smallest things such as drinking more water and moving your body can often have a significant impact on your wellbeing.

This is a reminder to look at how you are sustaining behaviors that support you, and stepping away from those which are unhelpful. All of us need that check-in when we have got back into the old ways of being, so remember this is part of the process.

KEY POINTS TO REMEMBER

- The only way comparison is useful is to help you see where to go next.
- If you spend too much time comparing yourself to others, you won't feel good or achieve your goals.
- Judgement of others is often judgement of yourself.
- It is easy to judge others if you haven't walked in their shoes.
- Compassion starts with yourself.
- We are all a work in progress.

12

Building for Long-term Success

This is it! I am hoping that you have made at least some small life changes, and you are starting to feel better. Recognize that it takes time to feel the benefits, but hold onto and celebrate the progress that you have made.

In this chapter, you will explore:

- Using your brain for the good
- The importance of reflection and growth
- Leaning into your energy and using this as a compass
- Practical relaxation techniques which will allow you to embed your learning

Keep in mind that you're always evolving and changing, even if it's unconscious. This is about being the very best version of yourself, and building new neural pathways so that you can change from the inside out and continue to grow – it's the secret of coaching. Coaching makes you feel better and now you have the tools to self-coach.

Your model for growth explores your current context – where you want to go, the path forward and then how to stay on that path. It is a powerful method for self-coaching; where you are, always considering how to move from where you are to where you want to be and making those small incremental changes to get there. With a review cycle firmly in place, you can make sure you are progressing in the right way, feeling good and getting the desired results. That is why the weekly CEO meetings to review your progress are so important (see page 182).

You can apply this framework to anything, whether it is finding a new job, learning a language or even finding love. You get super-clear on the desire, and then it is about designing the way that you will get there. The simple part is always the strategy: this is what you do. The harder part is making that strategy stick, and this is where we have looked at common pitfalls and things to avoid, focused on both your internal energy and environment.

This is what "the work" looks like – this continual commitment to exploring and learning about yourself, alongside accepting that you are all that you need to be right now. The more we work on ourselves, and build our own self-awareness, the more we can seek to understand others, build more effective relationships and communicate well. We are happier humans when we connect with others, without all the stuff that we carry.

If you take one thing away from this book, it is that we are all carrying a whole heap of stuff that may well be unhelpful for us in building the lives we desire. Our thoughts, emotions, behaviours and beliefs are all open to change, and the more that we know about ourselves, the more we can start on this journey.

Of course, the myth of instant change isn't real. We can't transform overnight – we don't suddenly become Polly Positive, if we have been Debbie Downer for the past 30 years. Change is not about massive changes – it's the small stuff: the daily step count, the weekly journalling, the moments of awe and wonder which make your heart sing. This is about initially integrating things into your life and your day-to-day and building on that.

Consider building your wellbeing like building a house brick by brick. Each small action when repeated, lays the foundation for change. Sometimes, it is tipping down with rain and maybe there is slow progress, and at other times it feels like you are flying.

Seasonal shifts

We hear about eating seasonally and how it is better for us and the planet. What about behaving in a way that is seasonal? There is some research that with the different seasons come differing demands. These may relate to the actual seasons or the feelings we associate with them.

For many of us, our progress is akin to the seasons. In the winter, we retreat and relax. We take time to sit with our thoughts and emotions, and we are naturally less productive; in fact, there is evidence that in winter we need more sleep and a suggestion that we should be working less.[20] If we work with our circadian rhythms, a slower pace in winter can help. In fact, we can go into "winter" energy at any time of the year; allowing ourselves to slow down and rest can be restorative.

If we use the seasons as a metaphor for how we feel in terms of energy, it can be useful. When you're in winter, your energy tends to be at it's lowest and you're likely to be at your lowest ebb; it's a time for reflection and introspection, when you feel like you want to be alone with your thoughts and emotions. Winter is often seen as a time to be at home and cosy; the whole Danish concept of "hygge" describes how you can create a warm and cosy atmosphere, and is often referred to as part of wintering. The author Katherine May talks about the concept of wintering and rest in her bestselling book *Wintering, The Power of Rest and Retreat in Difficult Times*. The idea of retreating into yourself and giving that time for reflection doesn't need to only refer to the season of winter.

Moving from winter into spring, we see the shoots of progress and it is often a time for sowing seeds. As we get more sunshine, we often feel optimistic and it can be a great time to start new projects and lay the groundwork and foundations for growth. The energy of spring is optimistic as we look ahead to the warmer sunshine-filled months. I often feel like I am stepping back into being sociable in these months, after some time hiding away, and can feel the energy of big projects or something new.

When we go into spring, we start to feel more confident and powerful again. Our energy is also higher, meaning emotionally and cognitively we are more engaged. It is a great time to be productive and often when you find yourself at your most creative.

In summer, we often slow down again – now it is about enjoyment and confidence. You can feel that summer energy, which has more of a playfulness about it and is linked to fun. In countries like the UK, summer is often seen as holiday season, with some places in mainland Europe effectively shutting down in August as the priority is fun and relaxation.

Finally, you head into autumn, a season where we reap the rewards of the work you put in during spring. In marketing and business, we always say you can measure success by what you were doing three to six months before and this is a similar analogy – things take time to bloom and grow.

Why is all this important? Well, if we are aware that the seasons can impact our mood, we can use them to prompt a check-in on what we are feeling.

What season are you in?

Answer the questions below to see what season you are in, and then you can plan what you do accordingly. Remember you are more effective when you work with your energy.

What does your energy feel like?
A - Fully energized
B - Feel like slowing down
C - Lower energy, more rest
D - At its lowest

How is your confidence?
A - Increasing
B - At its highest level
C - Starting to decrease
D - At its lowest

What is going on for you?
A - Feeling engaged, productive and ready to take action
B - Enjoying the vibe and taking it a bit slower
C - Reaping the rewards of your work
D- Wanting to rest and recalibrate

How are you feeling?
A - Excited and powerful
B - Confident and up for fun
C - More anxious and irritable
D - Reflective and introspective

Look at the answer you chose most of the time to work out what season you are in:

A - Spring

B - Summer

C - Autumn

D - Winter

Consider where you are and what you want to do. You can change your energy, but we are often more effective when we work with it.

Integration and being

As a trained energy coach, one of the things that I learned is that we need to integrate. I work with a methodology called 'The Spiral', which is based on clearing negative emotions that vibrate at different energies in different areas of the body. After each session, I work with my client to assess how integrated the work has been. I then suggest integration activities to embed the behavioural change; these are similar to the ones we have talked about in the book and tend to be:

- Journalling
- Walking in nature
- Meditation
- Yoga

As a trainer, I spend a lot of time supporting our trainees to work on "client growth". This competency is focused on what the client will do as a result of the coaching session, as the work outside the sessions is where behavioural change happens.

Often, this is around their own reflections and thoughts, as well as what they want to do next – for example, when we have had a session which has seen them recognize and notice shifts in their body, they often go for a walk or do yoga. If they have been working on something much more cognitive, then journalling or meditation may be more appropriate.

Integration is there to help people to reflect on and embed the learning. It is the process of giving it space and time to ensure we use it in the right way. It is the equivalent of cooking your ragu sauce for hours, so the flavours develop rather than a quick 20-minute job, which may taste OK but won't hold the energy and depth of flavour.

You need to marinate the information and learning, and then consider exactly how you will apply it so you are doing what is right for you and what your mind and body needs. As I have said before, this is the go slow, go deep approach, where you are considering how you can make the change on a cellular level, rather than just wallpapering over the cracks.

Reflection and growth

Like a flower, we need to have the right conditions to grow. Self-reflection helps us to identify what we need and how we may need to change the course of what we are doing. Equally, we need to feed our bodies and brains with good stuff. I am not a fan of banning things; I find it more useful to look at the ingredients which help us:

• **Hydration and water**: How often have you hit a slump only to drink water and feel good again? I find a shower/bath, or ideally a swim, is the very best cure for a hangover. I have no idea of the science – it just works!

- **Nutrition**: Eating things which resemble what they are – for example, fruits, vegetables, grains – we know the Mediterranean and Nordic diets are both good for our bodies and brains. The Mediterranean and Nordic diets are rich in plants, low in processed foods, high in legumes and wholegrains. Fish has been found to lower the risk of heart disease, type 2 diabetes and some cancers. The Nordic diet has a smaller pool of evidence but has been shown to be linked to lower rates of obesity and LDL cholesterol. For more information check out Mellor and Georgousopolu's review in *The Mediterranean Diet*[21].
- **Movement**: Ideally walking, running, cycling or swimming – whatever works for you. Outdoor activities are preferable to being in a gym.
- **Journalling and meditation**: Both activities create space and time to be more mindful. If these don't work for you, think about what else is in your toolkit.
- **Connection and love**: Spending time with the right people makes us feel better.
- **Education and knowledge**: Think about what you love to learn and learn it! Build your knowledge.
- **Rest and sleep**: Getting 7–8 hours sleep each night is one of the best things we can do for our brain.

When we have our toolkit, we can add and take away from it. Everything is about balance. You don't need to become a holier-than-thou person who never stays up late, eats McDonalds or gets in an argument. Human beings are fallible; we all have our shadows. I have done more personal development than you can shake a stick at, and I still have times when I don't feel like I have anything together.

The "be perfect" myth

Let's put this to bed right now. No one is perfect, your progress isn't linear and anyone you admire will have made more mistakes than you can ever imagine. The irony is we only get good at things through practice. Even though I have coached thousands of people, I still make mistakes and sometimes have some pretty ropey sessions. My baseline for good has improved, but there is always space to grow more.

If someone is suggesting that they are "perfect", and they never make mistakes, they are either lacking any self-awareness or they are surrounding themselves with yes people. You don't need to be perfect and you certainly will make yourself pretty miserable if this is your aspiration. Lower your standards and allow yourself to be content with good enough; you may well pleasantly surprise yourself.

You may be more prone to perfectionism if it is a core driver (look back at the Transactional Analysis section on page 198). Keep in mind, however, that when you have a growth mindset you can change the impact of these core drivers. This isn't about going cold turkey and no longer caring about how good the work you do is; it is about starting to lower your expectations and be kinder to yourself about where you are and what you have achieved.

Your energy is a compass

As you go on this journey of self-discovery, your energy starts to become your compass. By asking yourself and reflecting on what you need, you can move forward – for example, if you wake up tired, getting up and going to the gym may not be what you need. You may benefit more from having a hot drink and going back to bed. The more you get to know yourself, the more you can adjust your behaviour to play into what you need energetically. Start to use the compass.

This is the long game. I believe that energy is as important a currency as time; if we are feeling energized, we get more done. The more that you can tap into your own needs and use this, the happier and more productive you will be.

Managing stress and reducing stress

Stress is a part of everyday life and something that affects all of us. Whilst some stress is normal, if we are exposed to chronic and persistent levels of stress, it can affect our wellbeing in a variety of ways. Stress decreases our immune functioning, meaning we are more prone to illness, from cancer and heart disease to viruses and colds. Equally, chronic stress impacts our sleep patterns, and is one of the biggest reasons why people are signed off sick from work. On a cognitive level, stress impacts our ability to think clearly, make decisions and focus. Over time, this will have an impact on performance and productivity.

To live a happier life, there are a few things you can do around stress:

- Identify your stressors and consider what you can do to reduce the impact or reduce your exposure – for example, if you are feeling high levels of stress due to your morning commute, is there an alternative way you can travel? Or can you reduce the amount of days that you go into the office?
- Consider how you can deal with the stressor more effectively. Often, this comes down to what you can and can't control. During the purchase of our house (which took a year), I would often remind myself what I could and

couldn't control, which helped ease my nervous system and made me feel less stressed.
- Build up your toolkit of stress-management tools – for example, exercise, meditation, being with friends and hobbies. Think about what makes you feel good and activates the dopamine response system in your brain
- Practise mindfulness and active relaxation – do things that help you to unwind, such as yoga, breathing exercises, having a relaxing bath. Again, consider what works for you.

When you are able to manage both your exposure to stressors and your response to them, it can help make you feel better.

KEY POINTS TO REMEMBER

- Change isn't linear: working with your brain and behavioural change takes time.
- The season you're in can impact your energy and needs.
- Your energy can be a compass as to where you want to go next.
- Stress management techniques can support you to feel better.

Conclusion

Throughout the book you have explored how to support your own behavioural change, and the fact that this will take time and energy. You have looked at the model which you can use to self-coach:

Step One: Assess where you currently are
Step Two: Get clear on where you want to be
Step Three: Make a plan to take you forward
Step Four: Integrate and embed change

You won't need to look at all the exercises for each stage again. Now that you have an idea, you can go through the steps above and return to anything that you find helpful.

If you are ever stuck, the best exercise to get clarity is the Wheel of Life (see page 8): it gives that snapshot of where you are and will help you to recognize your first area of focus. Equally, it can be used as a starting point for Step Two. If you are stuck in Step Two, you can bring in your visualization/vision board activities or link back to the Be, Do, Have exercise. The planning stage, Step Three, is about opening up possibilities.

From a growth and behavioural change perspective, Step Four is the most critical: you now know that behavioural change takes time, so making a plan and then having those weekly

CEO meetings and check-ins to ensure it is being integrated is imperative. If you aren't making change by sticking to and building those new neural pathways through the compound effect of small behaviours, the rest of the work won't be sustainable.

This is a model and way of self-coaching which you can come back to time and time again. It may be that you use it at work if you are facing a difficult conversation, personally if you are making a decision or whenever you are feeling stuck. The easiest way to work through the model is to write your answers down to get clarity and notice patterns. Reflecting through journalling can also help you to acknowledge your thoughts and emotions, which can be beneficial in your decision-making process.

The more that you practise self-coaching, the more you will see that you have the power and knowledge that you need to move forward. Self-coaching has helped me navigate through the illnesses of loved ones, tricky personal situations and work dilemmas and has helped thousands of my clients. When you have this formula in place, it is a rinse and repeat process you can use to go underneath the iceberg and work with your unconscious, as well as your conscious.

If you want to feel better, then self-coaching is key. This inside-out approach to wellbeing means that you're able to think more effectively and solve problems. It's the reason the global coaching industry is the second fastest growing industry in the world and why people talk about how life changing coaching is. When you have the skills to coach yourself, you're able to take more ownership of how your life looks: this work is transformational. I'm so excited that you now have these skills and are able to integrate them into all areas of your life.

Acknowledgements

A special mention to the team who work so hard to support me at Optimus Coach Academy. The core team who have been incredible with leading training, assessing and mentoring whilst I write: Donna, Julia, Hannah and Fay; our admin support who make life so much easier: Sharron, Kellie and Debbie plus our contractors who support with training (and design): Bret, Jackie, Dawn, Lisa, Nicola and Carly. And to my marketing support squad: Haddy who is one of the best PRs out there, Christian who is my right-hand man and in charge of marketing too (I love you darling), Amanda and Rose who make sure I scrub up and look good in photos, Lynsay who edits my podcast and her husband Simon who does YouTube for me.

Plus, to all the people who have worked with us in the past and will do in the future: your support means a lot and I value you.

To all of the people I have worked with as a coach: my clients both in my personal practice and at Optimus and all of those in my communities. Thank you for trusting me and listening to what I'm saying – it means so much. And to my coaches and mentors who have supported me over the years: Shaa, Suzy, Susie, Taki, Phil, Noor, Emily and Alice – I appreciate all of you.

Thank you to all the team at Welbeck: to Jo and Beth, and to Dawn for all of your editorial support, and for the wider team for the design, distribution and all of the other pieces which go to making a book.

ACKNOWLEDGEMENTS

To the lady who made this all happen Jessica Killingley: who believed in me, pushed me and helped me to get this book into a shape to get a publisher and has been one of my most consistent cheerleaders – I appreciate you more than you know. I'm very grateful to you and the wider team at the BKS agency.

And finally to my friends and family: to my husband Christian (again) who looked after the kids, made me endless teas and coffees and is always on my side. To my daughters for giving me some peace and quiet. To my mum. And to my friends who I haven't seen as much when I've been writing the book and have always been there for me – I love you all.

Useful Resources

Books

Flourish: A New Understanding of Happiness and Well-Being – and How To Achieve Them by Martin E. P. Seligman. Nicholas Brealey Publishing, 2011.

Grit: Why Passion and Resilience Are the Secrets to Success by Angela Lee Duckworth. Vermilion, 2017.

Emotional Intelligence: Why It Can Matter More Than IQ by Daniel Goleman. Bloomsbury Publishing, 2020.

The 7 Habits of Highly Effective People by Stephen R. Covey. Simon & Schuster UK, 2020.

Atomic Habits: An Easy & Proven Way to Build Good Habits & Break Bad Ones by James Clear. Random House Business, 2018.

Tiny Habits: Why Starting Small Makes Lasting Change Easy by BJ Fogg. Virgin Books, 2020.

The Big Leap: Conquer Your Hidden Fear and Take Life to the Next Level by Dr. Gay Hendricks. HarperOne, 2010.

Life Lessons from a Brain Surgeon: The New Science and Stories of the Brain by Dr. Rahul Jandial. Penguin Life, 2020.

The Source: Open Your Mind, Change Your Life by Tara Swart. Vermilion, 2020.

Think Again: The Power of Knowing What You Don't Know by Adam Grant. WH Allen, 2021.

Mindset: Changing the Way You Think to Fulfil Your Potential by Dr Carol Dweck. Robinson, 2017.

Time to Think: Listening to Ignite the Human Mind by Nancy Kline. Cassell, 2002.

Seven and a Half Lessons About the Brain by Lisa Feldman Barrett. Picador, 2021.

Biased by Dr Jennifer Eberhardt. Windmill Books, 2020.

TED talks / videos

Grit: The Power of Passion and Perseverance by Angela Lee Duckworth. TED, May 2013.

The New Era of Positive Psychology by Martin Seligman. TED, Nov 2013.

Improving Our Neuroplasticity by Dr. Kelly Lambert. TEDx, Feb 2020.

After Watching This, Your Brain Will Not Be the Same by Dr. Lara Boyd. TEDx, Dec 2015.

The Surprising Habits of Original Thinkers by Adam Grant. TED, Apr 2016.

Thinking Fast and Slow by Daniel Kahneman. Talks at Google, Nov 2011.

Embrace the Near Win by Sarah Lewis. TED, Apr 2014.

Remaking Love by Barbara Fredrickson. TEDx, 2014.

Podcasts

Happy Place by Fearne Cotton

Unlocking Us by Brené Brown

Brain Science by Ginger Campbell MD

Feel Better, Live More by Dr Rangan Chatterjee

The High Performance Podcast by Jake Humphrey and Prof. Damien Hughes

Re-thinking by Adam Grant

References

1 Baikie, K. A., and Wilhelm, K. (2005). 'Emotional and physical health benefits of expressive writing', *Advances in Psychiatric Treatment*, 11(5), pp. 338–346. Available at: https://doi.org/10.1192/apt.11.5.338 (Accessed: 4 January 2023).

2 Forsyth, J. P. and Eifert, G. H. (2016). *The Mindfulness and Acceptance Workbook for Anxiety*: A Guide to Breaking Free From Anxiety, Phobias, and Worry Using Acceptance and Commitment Therapy. 2nd edn. *New Harbinger*.

3 Pillay, S. (2016). *The psychology of low back pain*. Available at: https://www.health.harvard.edu/blog/psychology-low-back-pain-201604259537 (Accessed: 4 January 2023).

4 Tseng, J. and Poppenk, J. (2020). 'Brain meta-state transitions demarcate thoughts across task contexts exposing the mental noise of trait neuroticism', *Nature Communications*, 11(3480). Available at: https://doi.org/10.1038/s41467-020-17255-9 (Accessed: 4 January 2023).

5 Ranganathan, V. K., Siemionow, V., Liu, J. Z., Sahgal, V., and Yue, G. H. (2004). 'From mental power to muscle power--gaining strength by using the mind', *Neuropsychologia*, 42(7), pp. 944-956. Available at: https://doi.org/10.1016/j.neuropsychologia.2003.11.018 (Accessed: 4 January 2023).

6   Ito, T. A., Larsen, J. T., Smith, N. K., & Cacioppo, J. T. (1998). 'Negative information weighs more heavily on the brain: The negativity bias in evaluative categorizations', *Journal of Personality and Social Psychology, 75*(4), pp. 887–900. Available at: https://doi.org/10.1037/0022-3514.75.4.887 (Accessed: 4 January 2023).

7   Kahneman, D. and Deaton, A. (2010). 'High income improves evaluation of life but not emotional well-being', *Proceedings of the National Academy of Sciences of the United States of America*, 107(38), pp. 16489-93. Available at: https://doi.org/10.1073/pnas.1011492107 (Accessed: 4 January 2023).

8   DiMenichi, B. C., Ceceli, A. O., Bhanji, J. P. and Tricomi, E. (2019). 'Effects of Expressive Writing on Neural Processing During Learning', *Frontiers in Human Neuroscience*,13(389). Available at: https://doi.org/10.3389/fnhum.2019.00389 (Accessed: 4 January 2023).

9   O'Connell, B. H., O'Shea, D. and Gallagher, S. (2017). 'Feeling Thanks and Saying Thanks: A Randomized Controlled Trial Examining If and How Socially Oriented Gratitude Journals Work', *Journal of Clinical Psychology*, 73(10), pp. 1280-1300. Available at: https://doi.org/10.1002/jclp.22469 (Accessed: 4 January 2023).

10 Madore, K. P. and Wagner, A. D. (2019). 'Multicosts of Multitasking', *Cerebrum*. Available at: https://pubmed.ncbi.nlm.nih.gov/32206165/ (Accessed: 4 January 2023).

11 Siedlecki, K. L., Salthouse, T. A., Oishi, S. and Jeswani, S. (2014). 'The Relationship Between Social Support and Subjective Well-Being Across Age', *Social Indicators*

Research,117(2), pp. 561-576. Available at: https://doi. org/10.1007/s11205-013-0361-4 (Accessed: 4 January 2023).

12 Hill, P. L. and Turiano, N. A. (2014). 'Purpose in Life as a Predictor of Mortality Across Adulthood', *Psychological Science*, 25(7), pp. 1482–1486. Available at: https://doi. org/10.1177/0956797614531799 (Accessed: 4 January 2023).

13 Johhannes, B. H. and Michael, E. (2020). 'Inducing positive affect and positive future expectations using the best-possible-self intervention: A systematic review and meta-analysis', *The Journal of Positive Psychology*, 16(3), pp. 322-347. Available at: https://doi.org/10.1080/17439760.2 020.1716052 (Accessed: 4 January 2023).

14 Vorhaus, J., Duckworth, K., Budge, D. and Feinstein, L. (2008). *The social and personal benefits of learning*: A summary of key research findings. *UCL Discovery*. [Online]. Availabe at: https://discovery.ucl.ac.uk/id/ eprint/10003177/ (Accessed: 4 January 2023).

15 Stickgold, R. (2005). 'Sleep-dependent memory consolidation', *Nature*, 437, pp. 1272–127. Available at: https://doi.org/10.1038/nature04286 (Accessed: 4 January 2023).

16 Philibert, I. (2005). 'Sleep Loss and Performance in Residents and Nonphysicians: A Meta-Analytic Examination', *Sleep*, 28(11), pp. 1392-402. Available at: https://doi.org/10.1093/sleep/28.11.1392 (Accessed: 4 January 2023).

17 Saghir, Z., Syeda, J. N., Muhammad, A. S. and Abdalla, T. H. B. (2018). 'The Amygdala, Sleep Debt, Sleep Deprivation, and the Emotion of Anger: A Possible

Connection?', *Cureus*, 10(7). Availble at: https://www.cureus.com/articles/13022-the-amygdala-sleep-debt-sleep-deprivation-and-the-emotion-of-anger-a-possible-connection (Accessed: 4 January 2023).

18 Walker, M. P., & van der Helm, E. (2009). 'Overnight therapy? The role of sleep in emotional brain processing', *Psychological Bulletin, 135*(5), pp. 731–748. Availble at: https://doi.org/10.1037/a0016570 (Accessed: 4 January 2023).

19 Ashforth, B. E., Kreiner, G. E., & Fugate, M. (2000). 'All in a Day's Work: Boundaries and Micro Role Transitions', *The Academy of Management Review*, 25(3), pp. 472–491. Availble at: https://doi.org/10.2307/259305 (Accessed: 4 January 2023).

20 Mattingly, S.M., Grover, T., Martinez, G. J. *et al.* (2021). 'The effects of seasons and weather on sleep patterns measured through longitudinal multimodal sensing', *npj Digitital Medicine*, 4(76). Available at: https://doi.org/10.1038/s41746-021-00435-2 (Accessed: 4 January 2023).

21 Georgousopoulou, E. N., George, E. S., Mellor, D. D. and Panagiotakos, D. B. (Preedy, V. R. and Watson, R. R.) (2020). *The Mediterranean Diet*: An Evidence-Based Approach. 2nd edn. Elsevier.

About Us

Welbeck Balance publishes books dedicated to changing lives.
Our mission is to deliver life-enhancing books to help improve
your wellbeing so that you can live your life with greater clarity
and meaning, wherever you are on life's journey.

Welbeck Balance is part of the Welbeck Publishing Group – a
globally recognized independent publisher based in London.
Welbeck are renowned for our innovative ideas,
production values and developing long-lasting content.
Our books have been translated into over 30 languages
in more than 60 countries around the world.

If you love books, then join WELBECK club and sign up
to our newsletter for exclusive offers, extracts,
author interviews and more information.

www.welbeckpublishing.com

🐦 welbeckpublish
📷 welbeckpublish
f welbeckuk